Malangatana

Malangatana Valente Ngwenya

EDITED BY
Júlio Navarro

Translated from the Portuguese by
Harriet C. McGuire, Zita C. Nunes and William P. Rougle

Mkuki na Nyota Publishers

To my parents
Manguiza Lima Ngwenya
Hloyasi Xirindya

To my wife
Sinkwenta Gelita Mhangwana

To my children
Mutxhini M. Malangatana Ngwenya
Hehlise G. Malangatana Ngwenya
Cecília Malangatana Ngwenya
Manguiza Malangatana Ngwenya

Published in English by Mkuki na Nyota Publishers
6 Muhonda Street
Mission Quarter, Kariakoo
PO Box 4246
Dar es Salaam, Tanzania

© COPYRIGHT
Malangatana and Mkuki na Nyota Publishers, 2003 (English edition)

ISBN: 9987 686 45 1

Originally published in Portuguese by Editorial Caminho, Lisbon, 1998
© COPYRIGHT
Malangatana and Editorial Caminho, 1998
ISBN: 972-21-1223-6
Legal Deposit: 127 681/98
www.editorial-caminho.pt

TEXT
Amâncio d'Alpoim Guedes
Frederico Pereira

José Craveirinha, Ulli Beier, Dennis Williams, Julian Beinart, Betty Schneider,
Francisco Bronze, Rui Mário Gonçalves, Eurico Gonçalves, Alvis Wottoun,
Cusa, Júlio Navarro, Mia Couto, Margot Dias, Gin Angri, Meira Visser,
Jorge Costa, Margarida Santos, Pablo Oyarzún Robles

DESIGN
José Serrão

JACKET DESIGN
Stained Glass Attempts, 1982
and details from
When They Arrived the Woman Was in That Condition, 1970:
The Child, That Hope, 1981: *September 25th*, 1983: *Yes, in the Deep of the Night,*
the Voices of the Women Scream and Sing, Announcing the Initiation Rites Celebration, 1983:
Nocturnal Secrets of Women, 1984: *The Exhausted Ones*, 1994: Untitled, 1998

DIGITALISATION OF IMAGES, FOTOLITO AND MOUNTING
CSS — Atelier Gráfico de Fotolito

PRINTING AND BINDING
SIG — Sociedade Industrial Gráfica

Editorial Caminho thanks Fernando Azevedo and Rodrigo de Freitas (directors of the Malangatana retrospective exhibit at SNBA, Lisbon 1989), and the Photographic Training Centre/Martinho, Maputo, and of Luís Silva, Lisbon. The Portuguese edition was supported by the Banco Commercial e de Investimentos, SARL, Grupo Caixa Geral de Depósitos.

Mkuki na Nyota Publishers acknowledges with appreciation, financial support from The Ford Foundation, South Africa, for the production of this English language edition.

Remembering the painter Malangatana Valente Ngwenia when he was still young

Amâncio d'Alpoim Guedes

During the 1950s and 60s there was something dynamic and extraordinary stirring in that most lovely city that the Portuguese built in less than fifty years, the city they called Lourenço Marques. There always were three distinct groups of intellectuals, artists, writers, journalists and poets in Portugal — those aligned with the powers that be, those opposed, and other who knew that the arts had little or nothing to do with politics. Mozambique lived in a closed and dreamlike world where there was only good news about the Empire, along with speeches and dedications. It was a world of rumours, secrets, news from the cafe and an ever-growing web of informant and agents — but where, in spite of all that, everything seemed possible. The various groups of writers, journalists and poets were reading, writing and translating the same things in the colonies as in the home country and in Brazil. When they tried to Africanise what they were writing, the result was always rustic and superficial.

In the final stages of preparations for the visit of the next-to-last President, the authorities realized that their new Airport Avenue traversed a long stretch of "Caniço" (the part of the city made of reeds) where the blacks lived in their flimsy miserable shacks of tin and garbage. To liven up the landscape for the VIP party who would be driving in and out of Lourenço Marques several times, some bright soul on the organizing committee passed out paint to the avenue's neighbours and there arose a fantastic display of painted walls and fences, a veritable outdoor museum of crude art, for a short time, that then passed away almost unobserved.

In the midst of all this, a young man serving in the kitchen and bar of the old Lourenço Marques Club, hub of the Portuguese society's elite in the capital, began to attract notice. He was drawing and painting at night at the Núcleo de Arte (Art Club) where his sponsor, Augusto Cabral, provided his paints and brushes to encourage his painting. This young man, Malangatana, had shown up at my studio two or three times, to ask that I draw up the blueprints for his house in Matalana, his hometown, out beyond Marracuene.

Malangatana was married and his wife was expecting a child. His manner of speaking was a patchwork of the upper-class arrogant phrases he heard in the Club's bar with a simple and graceful Portuguese, interspersed with English phrases and Ronga proverbs. This was how I first noticed his presence in a society in transition, little knowing that he would become a significant figure in that milieu within a few years.

One night Dori and I went to the Núcleo de Arte. We found Malangatana painting in the same room as José Júlio, a professional signalman and amateur painter then stationed in the city, who had taught him to use oils and to prepare the pressed wood boards that we all used to paint on. He had also turned to José Júlio to learn neocubist triangulations, which he immediately transformed into a very idiosyncratic style. The work Malangatana was then finishing was none other than "The Plant of Love" that impressed us profoundly.

Malangatana told us the story represented in the painting — a drama of love, jealousy and crime — in the following words: "There were two women married to the same man who got angry with each other one night. They grappled and one cut the other's leg with a kitchen knife. The one doing the cutting was the most jealous. And the one who had been cut, in spite of the wound, said this to her friend: 'I'm going to go away and take my lover with me to settle in another place.' And the one who had done the cutting, feeling very contrite, ran to get treatment which didn't work because the cut was very severe. That was how they broke apart. The plant is the plant of love." This narrative is typical of the explanations he used to give in those days — apparently simple stories that were almost parables.

But what impressed me even more was the extremely personal and confident way he had composed the painting, both in terms of shapes as well as colour.· In the lower right corner is an enormous knife, set with the point toward the maimed woman and rapidly moving to the upper left corner of the work where her left hand holds a small plant. The body of this woman is painted in such a way that she has turned around so that her face looks straight at us. Behind this woman is an enormous five-litre bottle, half full, that dominates the centre of the painting and relates to the big glass jar on the right — which is also the body of the other woman and on which her head is super-imposed. The face of this woman also looks straight at us, the same as the victim's did. The two staring eyes are linked by up and down lines, a mountainous and smoke-filled horizon that gives the painting great depth and fixes us within a plain, triangulated by light and dominated by a bright triangle, which he invented to accentuate the neck of the bottle and its central position. The colouring of the painting is sophisticated — dark clear reds, pinks from the same red and

also yellowish pinks and blues which, mixed with the reds, result in multiple tones.

I was enchanted by the painting and asked him to sell it to me.

Malangatana had never sold a painting. Days later, after consulting various people, he set a price. It was inconceivable how a simple beginner could design such a complex painting, so complex, personal and rich in pictorial effects with an ease that is rare in many master painters. Only later did Malangatana tell me that the story of the love plant was his mother's, wife of a man with other wives — one of the more serious human and social problems of Africa.

We also saw other 1959 paintings, which he still signed Valente or M.G. They were composed with differently scaled bodies and body parts. Sometimes one part of a face in profile or frontal on one side of the painting upset the composition or most particularly its scale. In others, he painted bodies or parts of bodies, bloodied — scenes of ritual monsters from his nightmares.

There were also paintings of a religious nature, a result of teaching and preaching in the mission schools Malangatana had attended, such as "The Virtuous Woman and the Sinner" and "Sacred and Profane Love", from 1959 and still signed Valente. In the centre of this painting is a nude young blond girl who looks straight at us while behind her, on the right side, a red woman, looking down, leans back on a Bible priced at 400 escudoes. On the left side, a dark yellow building topped by a cross appears. In the "Blue Woman, Crying" painting we see her, along with two other women, in a red interior space with some furniture and two small flying crosses. Through the windows one sees a series of churches, which are like his first paintings and drawings — urban landscapes with complicated and mixed up perspectives. I no longer remember the various stories that Malangatana told explaining the subject matter of the paintings that were, as always, somewhat in the style of church teachings, badly told.

There were also portraits that he painted such as "The Lady Going Shopping" that I have always called "The Pirate". The centre of the painting is filled with a monumental woman with a red scarf on her head, who looks straight at us, with a fixed crazed look that later would become one of the elements of a Malangatanan style or manner. On the left side there is another face which echoes the centre portrait and also looks fixedly at us. On the right side, in a receding plane, is a figure of a woman with a strange bottle superimposed.

The woman is clothed in a garden print cloth, with flowers and plants.

We bought some of the paintings that most interested us and we saw him frequently. He would show up at our house and at the studio, telling us what he had painted and what he was painting and showed us the drawings he then made with great spontaneity. These were extraordinary drawings, where the layout of future paintings was already defined.

One day I asked him if he would like me to speak to Grémio's president, Otto Barbosa, an old friend and client, asking that he be permitted to leave the Club prior to the end of his work contract so he could dedicate himself entirely to painting. I promised him a monthly income higher than his salary and also proposed that I buy one painting a month. If he wished he could set up his workroom in the garage next to my studio. He liked the idea, Otto Barbosa immediately agreed, and within days Malangatana had set himself up in the garage. I told him not to look at my books — they had nothing to do with him, that he was one of the best things happening in Mozambique, and that what he was doing was truly revolutionary. A day or two after setting up his things, he started working like a crazed person. He worked in the studio until eleven or midnight. Before going to bed I would see how his work was going — there were days when I got up and went down to the studio at eight in the morning, the hour when my workers arrived, and still I would find him working. In a little more than one year he painted some two hundred canvases and made innumerable drawings and studies. In those days South African artists, fellow architects and their students

used to visit me often; some students came to do internships with me. Professor Beinart, then living with us, became very interested in Malangatana's works; he took photographs and wrote an article which he sent to Ulli Beier, the editor of *Black Orpheus*, an art and literary magazine published in Nigeria. Soon thereafter Mr. Beier came to Lourenço Marques to meet us; enchanted with Malangatana's paintings, he bought several to organise a show in Nigeria.

Meanwhile a group of art and architecture students from Witswatersrand University and other artists asked me to organise a summer course with Beinart. Malangatana joined that course which we held in one of my buildings, then in its finishing stage. This was an extraordinary event locally, commented on daily in the local press. All these visitors were also very interested in Malangatana and his work, and their interest gave him immense enthusiasm.

Shortly after coming to my garage he began to write stories and poetry. The poems came to him with sudden inspiration, sparked by a newspaper item, a visitor, a dream or a nightmare. The stories were from his own life or the tales he used to tell. Some of these stories related to what he was painting, such as "The Story of the Letter in a Hat" which related a dramatic tale from Caniço in four paintings. The first two are vertical rectangles, the third is a square with each side equal to the larger size of the first two; the fourth is the same size as the first two, but painted horizontally. This arrangement of three equal-sized rectangles and a square, which portrays a scene just before the tragic end of the story, is a subtle one, permitting various ways to display the set.

The first painting is set at seven a.m. and shows Luisa's husband going to work, "The Husband departs, unaware that he carries his wife's letter to her lover." The door of the house is open and we see the back of his figure, contrasted against the golden morning sun. We see the letter tucked in his hat. Luisa is still sleeping, wrapped up in a sheet with a shoulder and part of her body exposed, which makes an eerie, drowsy response to the depiction of Luisa's face.

The face is accented by a dark blue triangle which brings the composition to life. The ripples of the sheet converge on Luisa's face; directly above it is a bedside table with a clock showing seven a.m., a rosary and a book. The perspective of the table is prolonged by an agitated series of triangles, converging on a small portrait of Luisa signed "Foto Sousa", which dominates the painting. At the right of the portrait is a window with greenish curtains, partially pulled back to repeat the triangles which animate the whole composition.

In the second painting, "The Husband's return with the lover's reply in his hat", we see Luisa, standing, nude with long, flowing hair, who uses her husband's exit to stage left as an opportunity to remove the lover's letter from the hat. Between the woman and the back half of the husband, we see a chair with a circular seat and, above it, the window, now with pinkish curtains reflecting the setting sun.

The third painting is the big square in which "While the husband sleeps, the wife hides a new letter for her lover". A dresser with mirror gives off a purplish reflection in the extreme left corner. Immediately above Luisa's back the chair with the circular seat appears, plus the clock and the rosary. In the top right corner we see the couple's bed, with the husband sleeping beneath the bedcover. A strong and complex diagonal movement, rising from the left to the right, dominates the painting.

The last painting, "The Husband's suicide, by drinking DDT poison, upon discovery of his wife's infidelity", is an agitated composition. The husband falls in an arch to the left, stuck down by the poison, while a ghost-like Luisa, seen in accentuated perspective from above, sleeps in the bed. Between the two we see a clock, marking three in the morning, a circular table topped with the poison, an illegible letter, a note on which is written "good-bye forever" and, over at the foot of the bed, there is a huge wristwatch, confirming three a.m. In the upper right corner we see a small portrait of the husband, which lights up this section of the painting. The painting is entirely broken up by triangulation and

the husband's head has a luminous contour. These paintings grabbed me completely by surprise, both for their quality and for the questions that arose regarding their roots.

These could have been comic books, or the steps of the Cross, or those primitive Italian lives of the saints, with successive events in the same paintings; Malangatana's astonishingly rapid assimilation of all influences at that time was evident.

The 1960 "Nude with Crucifix" is painted in shades of reds, oranges and yellows with a purple crucifix. The body is shown from a little below the knees up to the tip of the nose, which gives the painting a grand monumentality and repeats his skill with truncated figures, developed in 1959 paintings. The nude is a landscape where parts of the body appear as mountains and valleys. The composition is centred by the 4-paned window, by the triangles of the curtains, and by an intense orange that reuses the aforementioned triangulation. The crossed window-panes echo the crucifix perched between her breasts and a hand with three white pointed nails begins an undulating arm, which we follow to the shoulder and a cascade of fat forms that are breasts, chest and stomach. The mouth and chin are part of that undulation, with the huge mouth outlined on three sides by similar curves. The chain of the necklace attached to the crucifix forms two textured curves embracing and accentuating the chin, and the two nostrils, partially hidden by the frame, form a rhomboid made by two triangles with the nipples and navel. Later in 1960 upon our return from a long European trip, Malangatana gave us a work painted during our absence, dedicated to our trip and called "Secret Voyage". It is a painting full of naïf surrealism, where a beach has trees with faces, a luminous skeleton raises a bottle of wine, half a woman is giving birth, and with various apparitions, a marvellous plant, a face faintly sketched in the sky and portraits of my wife and me.

In the "Scene with Four Women and the Fetisher" the space is undefined and grayish, with two openings or windows in the background, a red fetisher in a trance appears in accentuated perspective linked to the centre window or opening above the left arm of a nude woman lying on a light blue rectangle. I always thought the subject was a birthing with the assistance of two female friends on the left side and the collaboration of a traditional healer on the right, who has at her side a half-filled bottle capped with a cup. It is a wonderful composition with arms, legs and other body parts animating the painting with gestures, inversions and dualities.

Many of 1960s paintings, like these two last-mentioned, are bigger than those he previously painted, covering the maximum size the slabs of unitext allowed. At the end of 1960 the garage was full of paintings, in spite of Malangatana having sold a good number. I counselled him to keep those he liked most because it was important to hold onto a good collection of his work for future reference and exhibitions.

We then began to think of a solo exhibition and, through the Nucleo de Arte, reserved the big room at the Organismos Economicos for April. Although Malangatana had worked intensely up to that point, he now began to work even harder to finish paintings, start others and organize the list of 60 works to be shown. At the last minute he wrote a short entry for the catalogue entitled "The Complete Painter" (27 - 29):

"These paintings are the product of a little more than one and a half year's work by a bar server. Malangatana is a natural and complete painter; composition and colour harmony are not intellectual games for him — they come to him as naturally as his stories and visions. He knows without knowing. His vision has uncanny parallels with European tradition.

"Some paintings resemble those of the primitive Catalans, other the macabre apparitions of Dutch visionaries, and still others come from a direct, magical and uncontrived surrealism. He apparently has inherited this tradition without having had access to it and without any instruction.

"He is visited by spirits; some paintings are hallucinations, fragments of an inferno already seen by Bosch. Malangatana has a profound knowledge of man's subterranean roots that, allied with his extraordinary formal vision, produces paintings with such rare totality that he is already one of the leading painters of Africa, in spite of still being a beginner."

The exhibition was a success. It was inaugurated by Commander Gama Rodrigues, representing the Governor-General, and many official entities were present. There were people who liked and bought, there were those who immensely liked but lacked the money to buy, there were those who doubted that it had been Malangatana who painted the works and supposed this was my joke, and there were those who didn't like anything about the paintings, nor about Malangatana, nor about me.

The night of April 24-25, 1961, shortly before the inauguration of the exhibit, Malangatana suffered a terrible toothache. In the morning, he went to the dentist who extracted a tooth. He went back to his studio with his face still swollen and painful, and began to draw the scene that he had just lived through. By the end of the afternoon he had finished "The Small Dentist", so-called because he painted a bigger one the next day. The painting is dominated by the figure of a dentist, whose enormous left arm holds the patient while the other hand digs in the bloody mouth. The face of the dentist is reflected on the head of the patient, which is supported by a light blue structure. On the left side of the painting there is a bowl in which a greenish tooth lies with a bloody thread. On the right side, deeper in the background, there is a dentist's table, full of tongs and pliers. This sudden transformation of a life experience into a work of art is proof of the speed and efficiency of Malangatanan talent, which operated without reference to any other works of art.

He also painted for the exhibit a "Scene of Sorcery", which is one of the first paintings full of people and animals which came to constitute the Malangatanan style, later painted on enormous canvasses and murals and copied by innumerable other artists. In the lower left corner of the painting is a big hand holding a paper or a mirror, above there is a yellow woman with blue hair whose left arm has been amputated and who is confronting two snakes. In the centre a fetisher with his back turned, bleeding from the neck; Dori and I are at one side and, just below, a yellow person is being eaten by a blue monster.

When the exhibit closed and the paintings which had been sold were paid for, he obtained a house in Canico, went to Matalana to fetch his wife and children, and from then on lived and worked in his home where I saw him almost every week. After the painted stories and his brief surrealistic adventure, Malangatana resumed painting his dreams, hallucinations and nightmares. Later in 1961 I mounted a vast exhibit of works by Malangatana, Abdias and others for the first International Congress of African Art that Frank McEwen had organized in Salisbury, Rhodesia. A little later I went to Ibadan, Nigeria, where Beier had mounted an exhibit with Malangatana's drawings and oils that he had bought on his visit to Lourenço Marques, where Beier's great interest in Malangatana's work had been sparked. I took advantage of Penrose's invitation to speak at the Contemporary Art Institute in London to organize another session on Malangatana, through which he became known in England. Beinart also was there and came along to speak about Malangatana. Later an enthusiastic critic organized a successful exhibit in London where all the paintings were sold. Unhappily the enthusiast kept all the money from the sale of the paintings. On June 6, 1961, Malangatana turned 25 years old. In less than two years of solo work he had been transformed from a bar server who painted at night to an internationally known and discussed painter.

There have been times when I've been introduced as one who discovered Malangatana. I always answer that Malangatana discovered himself. What I did was try to explain to him what it was about his drawings and paintings that was unique and extraordinary, and to give him the strength which I thought he needed for the transition voyage from his world to the incessant cannibalisation of cultures that the West engages in.

Speaking of Malangatana
Hearing Echoes of Matalana

Frederico Pereira

Speaking of Malangatana. Speaking of Malangatana the artist, painter, sculptor, poet, dancer...

Speaking of Malangatana... and one repeats this phrase as if it were an obsession, a stock-taking, a quest...

The truth is, all the same, it is so difficult to speak of Malangatana, that is, to speak of the inside (and it is not possible to speak of the outside, it is not possible *to comment.*)

It is not possible to speak of Malangatana's Art, ignoring the *person*, forgetting that special form of subjectivity that is embodied in the person, that presents itself to see and be seen at the same time.

Malangatana is in a special position, by his generosity, by his acute intelligence, by his super-acute sensitivity, by his skill in dealing with diverse worlds (complementary?); in *linking* diverse worlds. Simultaneous: the inside world and the outside world; that which originates from his subjectivity and that from which his subjectivity originates.

In our tradition, over here, Art perhaps constitutes itself as a negation, a negativity concentrated in being the subject that erects itself over what is presented as an original loss, a loss that no transformation can undo. Everything presents itself as a substitution, even when, in a paradoxical gesture, the Subject seeks to (re)encounter itself *around* the Object, *in* the Object, or even dissolving into the Object.

But in other contexts, the force of artistic transformation is greater when it is *interwoven* with the original, which, rather than experienced through the register of *loss*, makes itself known through a regime of a permanent (re)encounter.

In the case of Malangatana, this original is the Maternal Culture into which he plunges, roots himself, towards which he transports us, outside of which he would cease to exist.

It is the entwining of the Subject and the Original, this ever-present pulsating Awareness (not loss) found in Malangatana, in the Paintings as well as in the Drawings, in the Sculpture as well as in the poetry and surely in the Dance, under the sign of the movement, a double movement, as much from the Original to the transformed as from the transformed to the Original.

One also sees this entwining in the relationship between Malangatana and Matalana, his home town, which is dispersed and divulged through him. Matalana is Malangatana's passion, and anyone who has heard him describe it also falls in love with it.

It is not possible to think of Malangatana's Art while forgetting that between him and his Original Culture there is such close proximity between one's myths, stories and imaginary objects and the other's myths, stories and imaginary objects. We, from a distance, celebrate the difference in what is presented from the world we inhabit as purely individual expression, Malangatana gives us a feast of continual links and entanglements between the *self* and the world of *others*, of nature and of myths and fetishes — without which the self would be condemned to the narrower world of *himself* or to the "larger", but dead and deadly world of the commonplace.

There is certainly not in this (how could there be?) any trace of folkloric nor naiveté (I think it so strange when this word is applied to Malangatana...). On the contrary, that which Malangatana puts right up in front of us is the *universal value* of everything explained by the Original Culture, by making this (curiously, some say) *local.*

Original Culture made local is *Maternal Culture, Mother Tongue, Maternal Village...*

In an era so tiresomely full of *"global villages"*, repetitions and *"unique cultures"*, such constant reference to Origin, and specifically to what is truly *unique by its dissimilarity*, is a special attribute of Malangatana's Art, well shown in his peculiar way of more fully *understanding, feeling, living* the multiple relationships between the Particular and the Universal.

He has related to Rui Mário Gonçalves: "When I was assisting my uncles, who worked with fetishes, I would dream and go tell my mother about the dreams as soon as I woke up. I would dream of a cat that grabbed me, and I thought he was inside me. I would dream of a snake that wrapped around me, and believed that he was also there inside me... Later I painted many pictures at night. I used to sleep, have dreams, see monsters that frightened me and I would paint them".[1]

It is apparent that dreaming here has, in and of itself, a value of truth. The artist, confronted by this unique experience — truly unique, because the experience is not conveyed in recurrent dreams — has the wisdom not only not to think "it was only a dream", but also to not use the dream merely as a "source of inspiration". He does not *disqualify* this essential subjective experience, nor does he seek any non-experiential means of fleeing that which inhabits in him.

This, that which inhabits him, this primordial psychic mass is crossed by a process of transformation that, rather than stifling the proliferation of dream imagery that gives it form, even if this form is troubling, this form that is in turn transformed by the narrative addressed to the mother or by its elaboration on the canvas.

The dream is not pure, pure distress or pure fear, nor is it merely cleansing — an act of simply bringing to the exterior *something* internal.

What Malangatana is talking about here is a process of complete transformation and elaboration which, at the end, produces a narration, a painting, a poem.

It might appear, as a result, that the narration, the painting or the poem serves only to *exorcise* the afflicted one.

However, this is not about exorcism.

The afflicted one uses raw material from the Original Culture to express himself and, in this expression, finds a way to get around something that had been traumatic to himself. The Subject's personal fears are given form by the dream where they are associated with the myths that populate the basic culture; in doing so, these fears subside and are dissolved thanks to the intervention of these myths.

In Malangatana's case, however, one finds a subjectivity *rooted* in the original soil of the Grand Culture, the Mother Culture which, like the Mother to whom dreams used to be told, protects the Subject from his demons and nightmares, and at the same time provides him with themes and forms that take shape when transformed through his distinctively personal style.

Here, the phrase "take shape" is meant almost literally.

It is easy to see that Malangatana has a close relationship with the Body — as well as with the Gaze, to which Mia Couto has previously called our attention.

In essence, then, there are no culturally uprooted forms in his work. There are no bodies whose movements derive from purely private imagination. They all pass through, as stated before, the Maternal Culture which is, at one and the same time, both a Body and a transforming womb (this is where Malangatana's art acquires its profoundly communicative and relational dimension).

The poem "Exposition" speaks of the violence of the outside:

The black women from the lagoons
mounted an exposition
of paintings bare and sad

With their own bodies the artists
painted on the base of the reed wall[2]

In this poem, we're now interested in the movement of poetic metaphor: *"With their own bodies the artists / painted on the base of the reed wall"*.

Here, in the play of the metaphor, the image being interpreted has a projective/constructive dimension. The aspect of the dream which resembles a screen is present in the "reed wall" image — and that is where one "projects" the body being used "to paint".

The body that paints is the projected body that one finds again in the painting. Body that paints. Painting that is Body.

But what are these body images that *get into* the painting? They are no private images whose meaning must be painstakingly revealed, they have come directly from the Maternal Culture. Myths. Fetishes.

The *dream*, the dreamlike subsoil of Malangatana's art, appears to have two layers: one very personal, private, turned uniquely in and of itself to the interior of the dream; and the other which has been worked over, turned to the outside of the dream, composed of images offered and organised by the Maternal Culture.

The second layer is first directed toward the mother and later *put into shape*. The importance of the maternal function — the Mother and the Mother-Culture — is vital: not only does it permit one to go beyond the forms and themes

given by one's purely private world to encounter that which is nameless and faceless, but it also gives meaning to the themes and forms found in that world beyond. The Mother-Culture, therefore, has a transcendent function: it provides the shapes, it provides the process for transforming the shapes, it provides the screen onto which the shapes are projected, and it is the mechanism through which these shapes can re-enter the interior world from which they have emerged.

Outside of the Mother Culture, it is impossible to understand *this* Malangatana; I'd venture to say it would not exist. Neither with respect to the specific images put before us. Nor with respect to the process of elaborating these images. Nor with respect to the possibility of travelling with them to the world from which they have come.

Except in this way, how would we understand this poem, "When the Children Dream"[3], that could easily have been the basis for a painting:

You came here last night
and sat here or there
but Mother didn't see you...

"Mother didn't see you" — a watchful maternal function results in *this*, that from a dream, arrived here or there, *moving freely* in the dream, formless and voiceless, it let *this thing* come *here* or *there*, and *"it had fire in its hand"*, running *this way* and *that way*, *"jumping and flying"*: "hitting me" and *"eating my mother"*, and *"telling (me) not to say anything to Mother"*.

But *"the children never lie. They tell the truth without knowing that it is the truth"*. Thus it is for each one in his dream, thus for Malangatana in his art: Above (or beneath) all, it is about Truth and Lies.

The dream does not lie and cannot lie: the dream simply exists. That is how it is depicted in the painting or drawing or what the poem says. Truth? Lies? Where did this strange thing come from? What does it mean? It hardly mat-

[2]Malangatana. *Twenty-four Poems*, ISPA, 1996, Lisbon [ed. note – poems were first published in Mozambique in 1960]
[3]*Ibid.*

ters: *"The children never lie. They tell the truth without knowing that it is the truth."*

The children recount what they see during the night. And *this thing* they see at night is more important than the daylight version: what they see at night comes from the same place as the daylight version, and the daytime version cannot be simply read superficially, with nothing spilling over to one side or the other. It is not correct to say that what was seen in sunlight is an alternative form of what appears in the dream: *what is in the dream is one's own, that can be found again in the visible world.*

And the children, in fact:

> *"go on telling a story*
> *when, miraculously, the dream*
> *appears to them.*
> *In reality they scream for mother*
> *and pointing say: what I saw is this"*[4]

The dream, therefore, appears itself in the real world. This dream corresponds to that layer of the dream constructed from stories and myths, it comes from them and leads toward them.

This dreaming is a projection of what feeds the legendary reality, or even the daydream, seeing how strongly the myth and the dream are interwoven.

Is it not the Mother Culture that gives birth to the conceivable, visible, dreamable part of the Dream? The space that *shelters* private psychic moments, the space for transformation — that is, in fact, in and of itself the primary maternal function.

One of its objectives appears to be: to hide that which is nameless and faceless, that which would be pure terror if it were not transformed and prevented from coming to the surface, that which is not meant to be seen, nor spoken of, that for which there is no space.

Malangatana's paintings dive down into this maternal-cultural-dreamlike space, where *our* disconnects between day and night are hidden in broken down (or, better put, unconstructed) form and therefore also have the "objective" of preventing these other nameless and formless

monsters from taking shape, name or place, because nothing — neither canvas nor dream — could possibly accommodate them.

Other-monsters would necessarily be afflictions and manifestations of a pure "I" as a negation and distance, fluttering around without roots.

One thing that fascinates me about Malangatana is how his art goes beyond *individual expression* to also, at the same time, *relate, communicate, share* a collective space so full that almost no canvas is able to encompass it.

In spite of the multiple things that "flutter about without roots", Malangatana would say no, *not that*. Or, better put, it might be said, this can never arrive at a true state of being *from this point hence* from which one would then draw back.

This is because Malangatana's world is a world of *roots*. Roots that, in the multiplication of their movements, let Malangatana be Malangatana. Nothing, in fact, is more solid than the on-going, ever visible, identification that he maintains with his *others*, that which exists *with his others* and comes *from his others* and what is built around the myths and woven in with the myths. This is also a source of fascination for us. And, because we might not be already aware of the movement associated with that being, we are ever lost in untangling subjectivities — and, with them, alternative identities — trying to *construct* one *unique* killer myth, the myth of Absolute Communication, whose mastheads in the end turn out to be mere *repeaters* of mutual echoes, which, I mean to say, neither communicate nor put the horizon in effective perspective... Of a Relation.

Malangatana, on the other hand, lets us feel an omnipresent Relation, the relationship of the whole to common roots, made up of shared individual spaces in relationship with an *alternate* where the other as well as the self reign in different regions.

The rhythm in the space of a plural Relation, the shared and the different, is fascinating to us and a source of enchantment.

The shared space — the space of the Mother-Culture — allows each one *to be* and at the

[4]*Ibid.*

same time protects it from distressing peculiarities. In Malangatana's paintings and drawings, this protection is extended by avoiding unfilled-in space, by avoiding the void.

Out of these spaces, and out of their various intersections, you could arrive at the world of unformed shapes, pre-formed shapes and precisely that which the shapes are trying to protect. In certain cases or situations, even the drawing method shows an involvement in a peculiar struggle with the void; it is not often in Malangatana's work that a design appears to be coming out of white space; rather, they start from a dark ink spot and take off from a leaf where nothing previously existed. In the expansion of the brush stroke, the drawing takes form: filling it in generates the contents; from there on, something is always bursting forth from something else.

In Malangatana, empty space does not appear to count even as potential space, rather it appears to have previously been space contested between the unspeakable and the untellable, something with no potential of being transformed into a form.

The World of Malangatana surely is a world nourished by unknown internal regions, but it is more than anything else a World oriented toward *the externally shared world*. From there on, the ocular function is important; in each painting, multiple eyes look out from diverse shapes and look at us while we look at all this, looking for the artist who gave them shape in the first place, and seeing himself in these forms as well.

There is also the importance of narrating the dream and the dream must be heard — to also hear the dream is to confer reality on it.

In "When the Children Dream," the artist-poet says:

*When the poor among them dream
they introduce much sorrow
principally when we don't link anything
during the telling of the tale*

The importance of giving form to the dream, and making that form visible — and understood, which is to say, once more steeped in maternal culture.

The private subjectivity of the artist no longer belongs to himself, he becomes the victim instead of a creative force, and this self-abandonment is determined by culturally significant figures.

The poem "The Owl" is very illuminating on the significant relationship with the void — and of the emptying of a form.

*The owl augurs for me
and tells me that I'll never arrive
beyond where desire leads me
and thus the dream evaporates
[...]
I am struggling with myself alone
it is impossible to conquer the waves
scratched over me through witchcraft
by the owls, cats and drums*

This space, this region of "myself alone" is preventable emptiness. The internal layer of the dream is covered by an external layer, populated by derivatives of the Mother Culture. Can there be anything more terrible, in the subjective view, than an empty dream, a dream that no one sees, not even the dreamer? He could fall precipitously into the emptiness, and monsters could emerge from the emptiness — killing the dream as well as the dreamer. His solitude is empty, because alone he will not be able to overcome the "bewitched waves" that are "evaporating his dream"...

Once again the center post is his anchorage in the Mother Culture. Within it, he is not alone; within it, the artist will no longer "evaporate".

The "matalanismo" of Malangatana can be understood from this point. Born in Matalana, Malangatana transmits a passionate force for the benefit of his village: passion for a reality that is also a dream. "The life-blood of his people", Julio Navarro has called it.

Malangatana does not only paint under the influence of dreams, he also starts from a half-dream, with the *sounds resonating from his village*. The sounds "are not human voices, but the noise of the wind on the leaves of the trees, the crowing of a rooster, and a silence that can only be African", Marco Vanotti tells us.

How the sounds of that birthplace, through what is almost fusion (but never confusion) become part of the hand that paints, the ear that hears and the ideas that are thought, is a peaceful transformation that permits a special kind of subjectivity to evolve — that of the Other, particularly the colonial Other, whose very differences make it possible to affirm what has been experienced in one's own soil.

This affirmation is found in the paintings, the drawings, the art of movement — and in the same manner is found in his poetry, with illuminating force.

And since that which is *rooted also is root*, the artist's subjectivity is mobile, not at all rigid (since rigidity is always defensive), achieving a capacity to identify less distinct subject positions, and from that point, becoming ever more human, ever more enriched with a larger vision of himself and the World, and the Myth which is the World.

In the poem "Song of an Old Man" this becomes not only visible, but also palpable:

Oh Lord, oh lord
oh boss, oh boss
I want to rest
my shoulder is hurting
my hands hurt a lot

In this poem, the artist identifies himself with the Old Man because of his way of looking at himself and the world, the positioning of his subjectivity gives space for this to happen, the same way that saying "this was what I saw" frames the space where it takes place:

Oh Lord, oh Lord
I have to walk
but my leg hurts
it hurts to walk Ningui-style
to walk one year and more
the sedan-chair doesn't weigh much,
but the white man does

The poem appears to be a complaint and is more than a complaint, but all the same is a complaint... This poem *is* and *is not* a complaint.

One subjectivity, that of the poet, internally differentiated and compartmentalized, identifies itself with another subjectivity, one that indicates its nature, movements and respective contours.

In "The Song of the Old Man", the Old Man in effect *makes himself present*, starting with a Gaze that he makes very much his own.

In the Poet's identification with the Old Man, there is *pure revelation* of the feeling and living Old Man with whom the poet could identify, but who he will not confuse himself.

And, together with that revelation, is the revelation of the colonialists' brutality and violence, shown with maximal clarity, without any unnecessary adjectives.

The same can be seen in many drawings whose titles simply speak for themselves: "The Carriers", "The Starving Family", "The Stevedores", "Shovel of Zampungana" and thousands of others.

Returning to the poem, one must add that there is no confusion between the Poet and the Old Man, the Artist and many Old Men, the difference in the identification is not constituted through violence.

Obviously this is not to say that violence can't be the ultimate means by which one's Subjectivity sets itself apart, affirming itself by radical denial of the Other who one intends to suffocate.

Meanwhile, Malangatana has other resources: he is capable of making an object out of the violence of the Other, keeping himself within his own subjective self.

Able to identify himself with the Old Man (Men), he is not led to also identify with that other face, the "lord boss".

The same could be said of poems such as "At the Polana" or "The Penguin Bar".

Malangatana counterpositions his irony to the violence of the Other, without incorporating brutality as a possible reaction.

Irony is a subtle form of critical distancing and of radical denunciation, but once again, he does not at any time slide toward *simpler* positions, such as sarcasm. In sarcasm, the subject assumes a destructive position against that which it intends to destroy. It gives continuity to evil from the outside, repositioning it in an apparent regime of transformation on the inside. That's where irony is transforming and sarcasm is essentially bred.

It is this singular form of irony — that which is truly distancing and differentiating — that one encounters in "The Penguin Bar", even in the rhythm of the words:

So much Mister
so much Client
so much tray
to serve Mister Client
[...]
so much drink,
so much sandwich
so much tobacco
all for Mister Client

And at the end, in sharper punctuation, indicating violence coming from the outside:

so much asking
so much sign of the early dawn
so much promise
that is for Mister Client

Violence that exists outside and stays there, is now *pointing objectivity and visually* towards the design of "The Penguin Bar".

Malangatana's Gaze could reveal the World's violence, but he was not the one who constructed this violence.

This gaze does not use violence (nor sarcasm) because doing so would correspond to insufficient autonomy of the Subject and an equally insufficient Objectivity of the otherworld.

Here in the paintings, as in the drawings, before dealing with the rooted Subjectivity — rooted, as has been said, in its own world, in its own origins, with these multiple gazes passing over, that are always heard and relayed — their own movements sustain the Subjectivity and are raised to larger and more universal positions.

It is this *subjective security* that makes the *objectivity* of the painter's and poet's gaze. And it is equally sure that this gaze was contaminated by the intolerance, brutality and violence that the history of the colonial experience inflicted.

All this happened because Malangatana's Art was born in a space neither real nor imaginary, but permanently oscillating between the two, in a world that resources provided by his roots made him able to see and describe, the dream world where he was himself anchored by his own roots in the dream.

And so we recall:

When 4-year olds dream
the children tell stories,
saying what came to them in the night
[...]
the children never lie
they tell the truth without knowing
that it is the truth

Whether the dreams are "bad" — nightmares — or "good", the scene where they are set and the Relation that is woven between it and the World is not a simple, neutral surface — rather it contains the homes of all that make the world a World.

This is why the painting, and the drawings, the poetry and the sculpture, are without end and don't fit on the canvas.

Being universal — and because it is universal — he reflects and constructs a world in which we see his people. As Lindo Nhlongo said: "The people began a real awareness of their life when they saw scenes from their everyday occurrences in Malangatana." However difficult they are for us to understand, the "stories of his people, the value of the legends and the fetishes of his community" take form in the paintings. Not only — and not most importantly — the monsters and fragmented bodies. Lindo Nhlongo goes on to say: "Malangatana's paintings have scenes of life, of happiness, sadness, pain and hope. Even in the paintings of great suffering and enormous despair, there is always a flower, a bird of peace or a pregnant woman symbolizing the hope and continual rebirth of the world.

Malangatana is, in the end, Malangatana and, at the same time, more than Malangatana: he is also Oblino, Lindo Nhlongo, Filipe Maxiana and many others: *he is all the people of Matalana.*

In his arts, Malangatana does not *speak* to us of any world, after all. He is perhaps more than this, he is a *magical presenter* of a World.

This is because Malangatana was made this way — and always seems to me, beyond the forms and the rhythms, a serious *person,* every time we meet.

Thus he was made, with an enormous capacity *to hear,* an enormous capacity *to see,* an enormous capacity *to gather.* I don't know yet how to bring in this other capacity that appears to me fundamental: tolerance, surely; authority, without doubt — but on top of all this, and perhaps as a basic condition for all this, *benevolent* with the *capacity to love.*

Malangatana

The Works

A Mulher Azul Que Chora
<u>*The Crying Blue Woman*</u>

1959

A Virtuosa e a Pecadora
The Virtuous Woman and the Sinner

1959

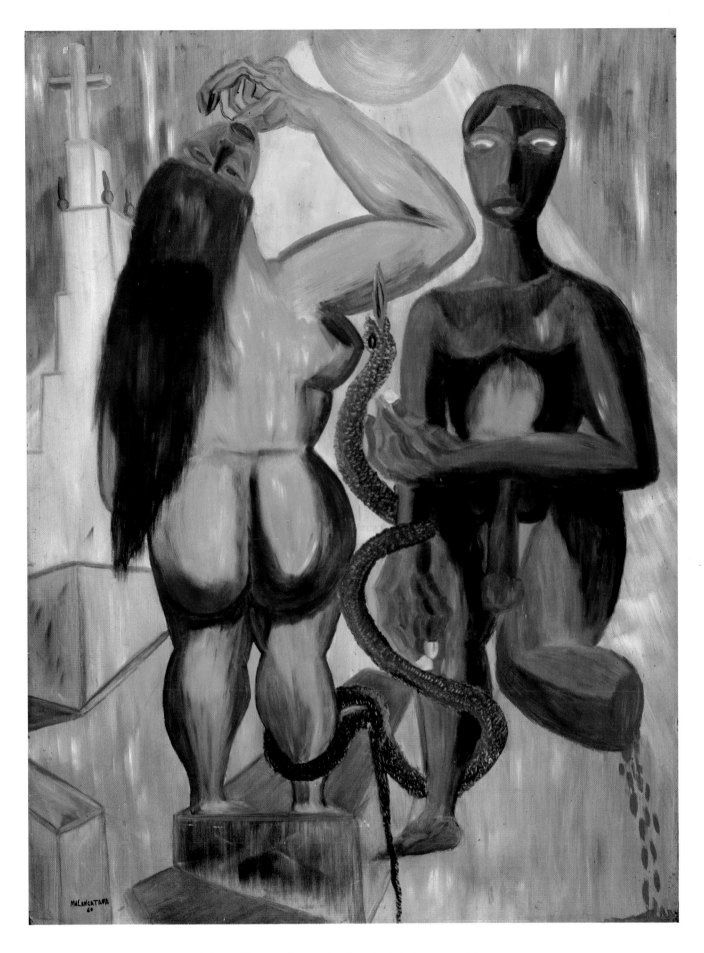

Adão e Eva em frente da Catedral de Lourenço Marques
Adam and Eve in Front of the Cathedral of Lourenço Marques

1960

Adão e Eva
Adam and Eve

1960

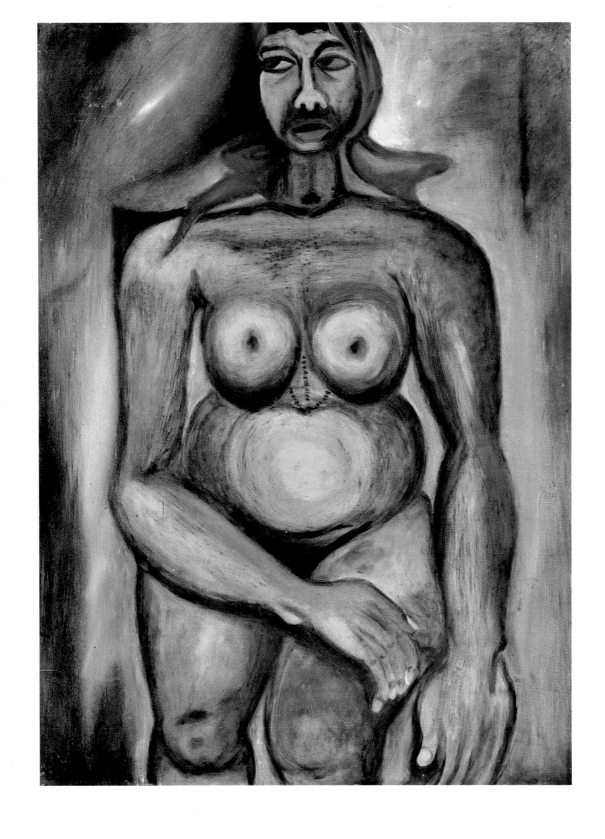

Nu Grande de Luísa
Luísa's Large Nude
undated

I

II

História da Carta no Chapéu
<u>*Story of the Letter in a Hat*</u>

1960

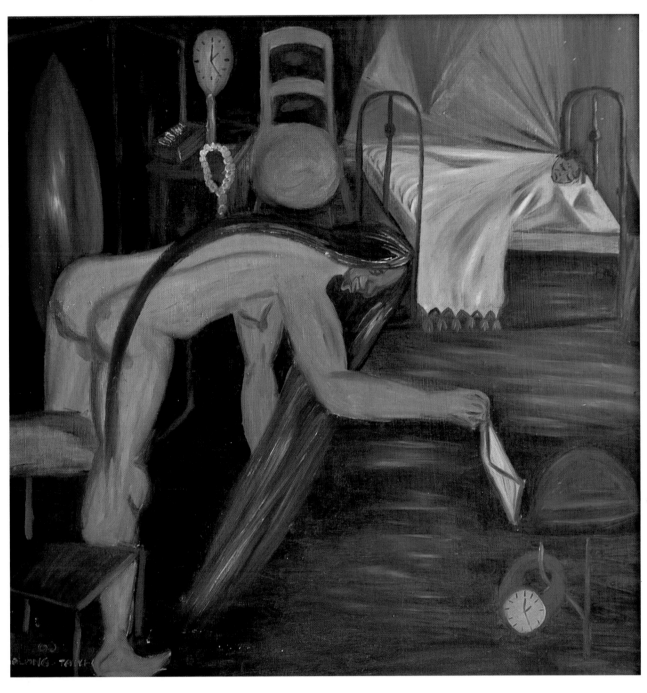

III

IV

Sem título
Untitled

1960

A Viagem Secreta
The Secret Journey

1960

A Menina Perdida
The Lost Girl

1960

Os Trabalhadores
The Workers

1960

Cena com Quatro Mulheres e Feiticeiro
Scene <u>with</u> <u>Four</u> Women and a Fetisher

1960

Nu com Crucifixo
Nude with Crucifix

1960

O Dia do Divórcio
The Day of the Divorce

1960

A Cena da Adivinha

Fortune Telling

1961

A Última Ceia
The Last Supper

1961

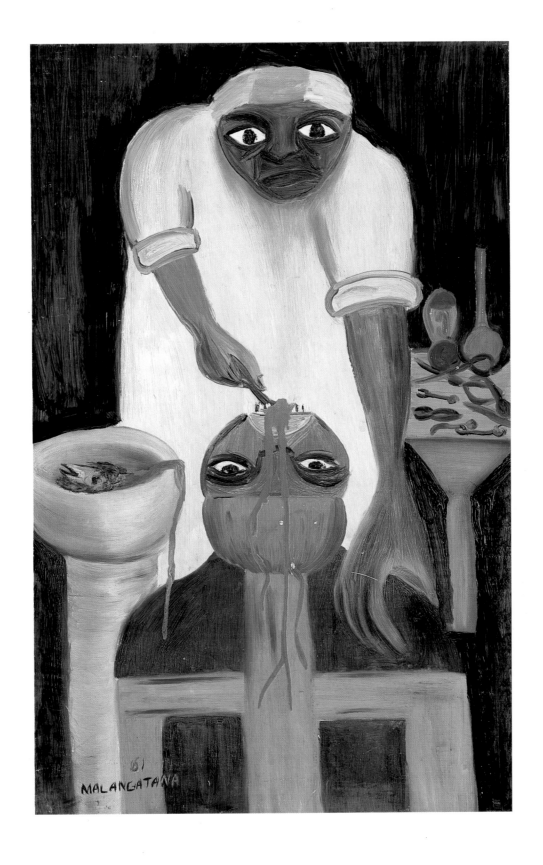

O Dentista Pequeno
The Small Dentist

1961

Juízo Final
The Final Judgement
1961

Monstros Grandes Devorando Monstros Pequenos
Large Monsters Devouring Small Monsters

1961

Zucuta
Zukuta

1961

Cena de Feitiço
A Scene of Sorcery
1961

A Feiticeira e o Mocho
The Sorceress and the Owl
1961

Primeiros Sinais em Nangololo
The First Shots in Nangololo

undated

O Trabalho Forçado
Forced Labour

1962

Carregador
The Porter

1962

O Adivinho, a Serpente, o Olho Visionário
The Soothsayer, the Serpent, and the Visionary Eye

1962

Abismo do Pecado

Abyss of Sin

1962

O Trabalhador com o Coração de Fora
The Worker with his Heart Exposed

1962

O Feitiço
The Spell ⟶

1962

Olá
Hi there

1963

Estrada das Lagoas
Lagoas Road

undated

O Estivador

The Dockworker

1963

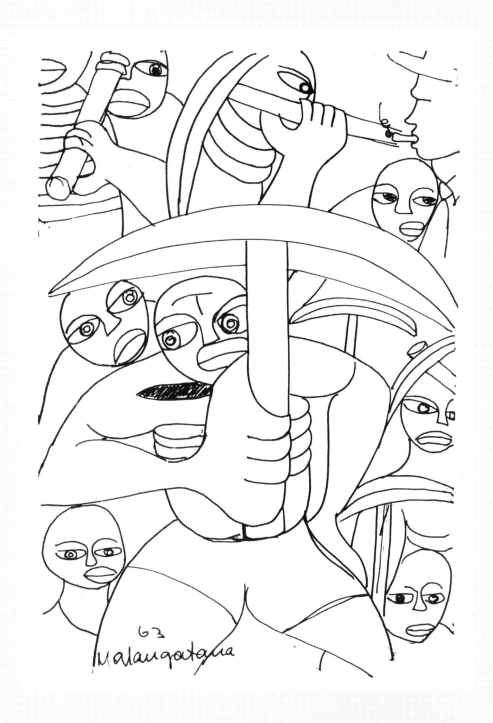

A Picareta
The Pickaxe

1963

Zapungana
Zapungana

1964

Sonho do Prisioneiro II (Preso Visitado)
The Prisoner's Dream II

1964

... e Auto-Retrato
... and Self-Portrait
1964

Despedida para a Guerra
Sending off to War ..
1964

Switukulu-mukhumba I
The Harbinger of Bad Tidings I
1965

Switukulu-mukhumba II
The <u>Harbinger</u> of Bad Tidings II
1965

Sonho do Prisioneiro
The Prisoner's Dream
1965

Sonho de Amor na Cadeia I
Dream of Love in Prison I

1965

Sonho de Amor na Cadeia II
Dream of Love in Prison II

1965

Sonho de Amor na Cadeia III
<u>*Dream of Love in Prison III*</u>

1965

Sonho de Amor na Cadeia IV
Dream of Love in Prison IV

1965

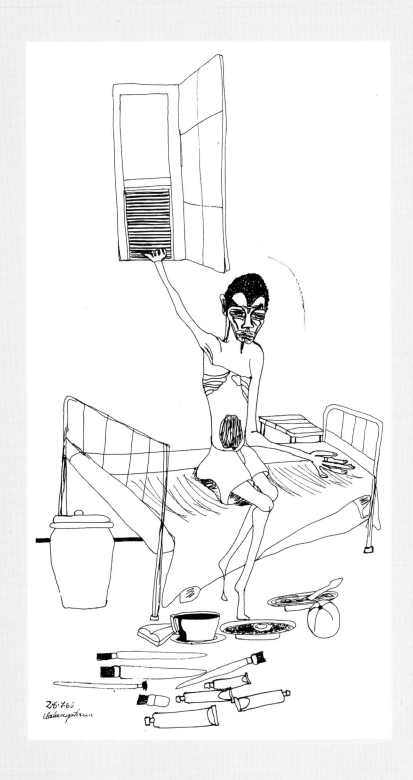

Prisioneiro
The Prisoner
1965

A Ciumenta

The Jealous Woman

1965

Calcinados
The Cremated Ones

1965

Cela 4
Cell 4

1965

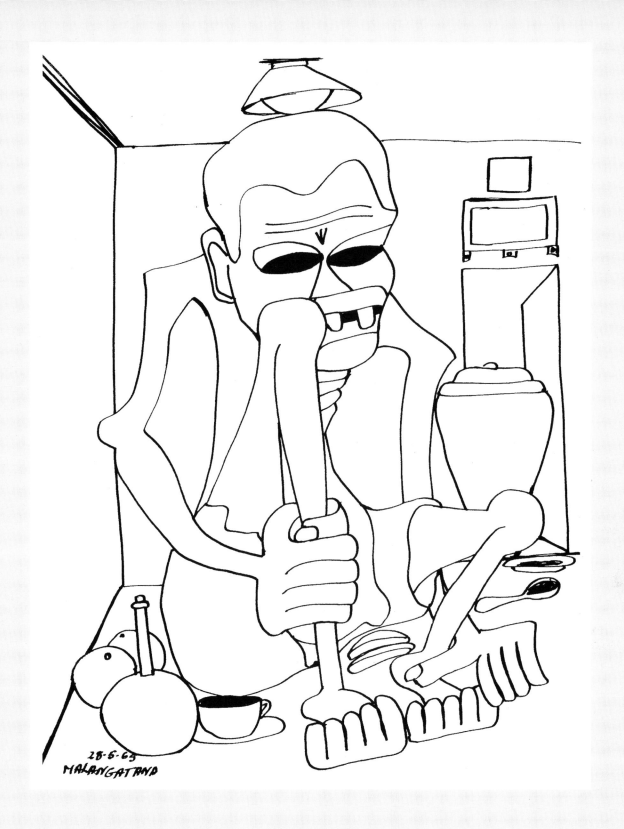

Cela Disciplinar I
The Punishment Cell I
1965

Natureza-Morta

Still Life

1965

Flautista Cego
Blind Flutist

1965

Parto na Cadeia
Childbirth in Jail
1965

Sem título
Untitled
1965

Julgamento de Militantes da Frente de Libertação de Moçambique
The Trial of Militants of the Liberation Front of Mozambique
1966

Pavilhão da Machava
The Machava Pavilion

1967

Cela 4 – Expectativa
Cell 4 – Expectation

1967

Crianças
Children

1968

Três Irmãos Cegos de Matalana
The Three Blind Brothers of Matalana

1968

Ceia

Supper
1969

Momento de Festa
Party Time
1969

Cela Disciplinar
The Cell for Punishment

1969

Quando Chegaram a Mulher Estava assim
When They Arrived the Woman Was in That Condition

1970

Loucos Não Me Toquem
Madmen, Do Not Touch Me

1970

O Saco Que Carrego É Branco como a Barriga dos Meus Olhos
The Sack I Carry Is As White As My Eyes' Stomach

1971

Nu com Frutos

Nude with Fruits

1971

Sem título
Untitled

1971

Flauta Mágica
Magic Flute
1971

O Amor e a Guerra – Yowe, Cântico de Um Guerrilheiro
Love and War – Yowe, Song of a Guerrilla Warrior
1971

Mãe África
Mother Africa

1972

Sem título
Untitled
1973

Gogwe-Cabra-Cega
<u>*Gogwe – Blindman's Bluff*</u>

undated

Três Peças de Cerâmica
Three Ceramic Pieces

1973

O Filho da Lenda
The Son of Legend

1973

A História do Pastor Zedequias Manganhela
The Story of Pastor Zedequias Manganhela
undated

Mulher

Woman

1973

Se Pensas/Que Me Deixas Petrificado no Solo/como Um Inútil/
/Enganas-te pois Meninos Crianças Nascem Todos os Dias
If you think/That you leave me paralysed on the ground/Useless/
/You are mistaken because young boys are born every day

1973

Quando Esse Peso Me Chega, Tomo a Figura mais Animalesca Que Todo o Homen Tem
When Life Weighs Heavily, I put on the Animal Form that resides within us all

1973

Polícia de Choque nos Subúrbios de Lourenço Marques
The Shock Police in the Suburbs of Lourenço Marques

1973

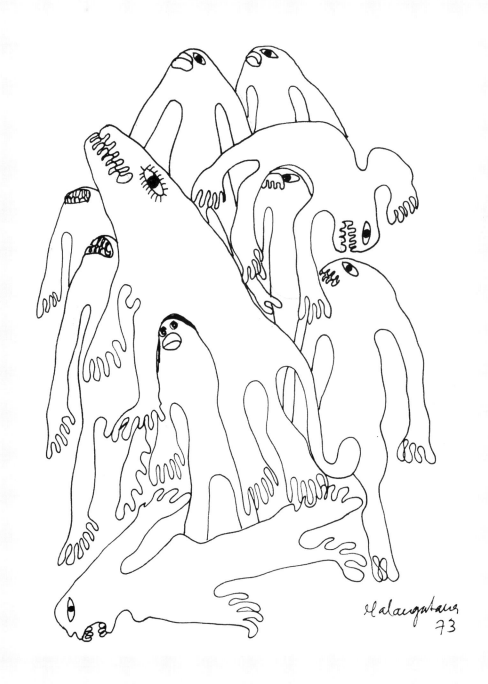

Uivar

Wailing

1973

Cesariana
Caesarean Birth

1974-1975

Lembras-te Daqueles Que Entravam a Sangrar?
Do you Remember Those who Entered Bleeding?

1974-1975

Minha Flauta Cantando/as Mil sem Fim/Canções da Liberdade I
My Flute Singing/The Thousand Songs of Liberty/without End I

1972

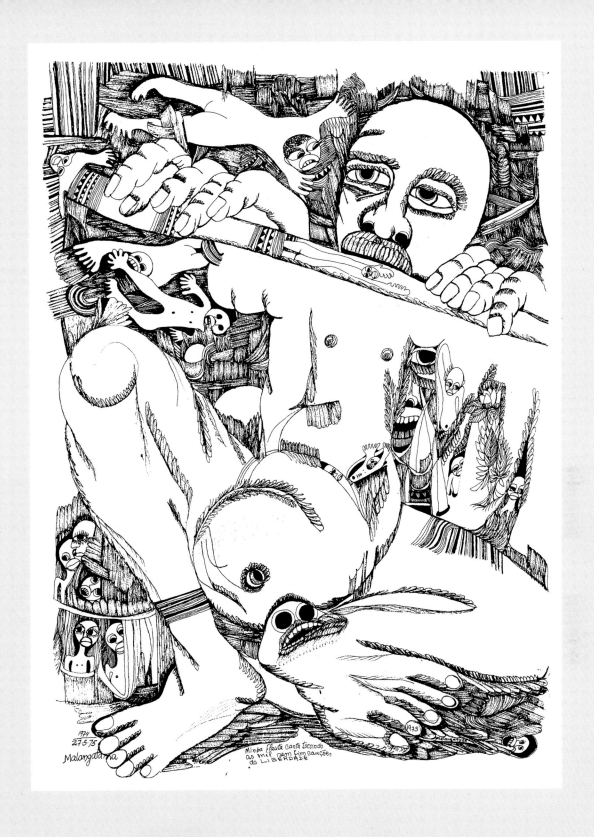

Minha Flauta Cantando/as Mil sem Fim/Canções da Liberdade II
My Flute Singing/The Thousand Songs of Liberty/without End II

1975

Os Três Bichos da Mulher e a Lua Verde Numa Noite em Que o Céu Era Azul
Three Animals in the Woman and the Green Moon on a Night When the Sky was Blue

1975

Banho da 1.ª Lua
Bathing in the First Moon
1977

Carta à Gelita II
Letter to Gelita II

1981

A Criança, Essa Esperança
<u>*The Child, That Hope*</u>

1981

O Desenvolvimento da Vida
Life's Evolution

1981

Terra Movediça

Quicksand

1981

O Aberto
The Opened One

1982

Mural
Mural
1982

Tentativas Vitrálicas
Stained Glass Attempts

1982

Sonho
Dream

1983

Sim, no Auge da Noite as Vozes das Mulheres Gritam e Cantam Anunciando a Festa das Primícias
Yes, in the Deep of the Night, the Voices of the Women Scream and Sing,
Announcing the Initiation Rites Celebration

1983

Minhas Máscaras
My Masks
1983

Yaka — Constróis!
Yaka — Build!

1983-1984-1985

25 de Setembro
September 25th

1983

Retrato Imaginário
An Imaginary Portrait
1984

Ritos de Iniciação
Initiation Rites ➤
1984

Primícias
First Fruits

1984

Segredos Nocturnos das Mulheres
<u>*Nocturnal Secrets of Women*</u>

1984

143

*O Longo Percurso
de Um Povo*
*The Long Journey
of a People*
1984

Do Outro Lado do Rio
On the Other Side of the River
1985

Cena de Amor III
Love Scene III
1985

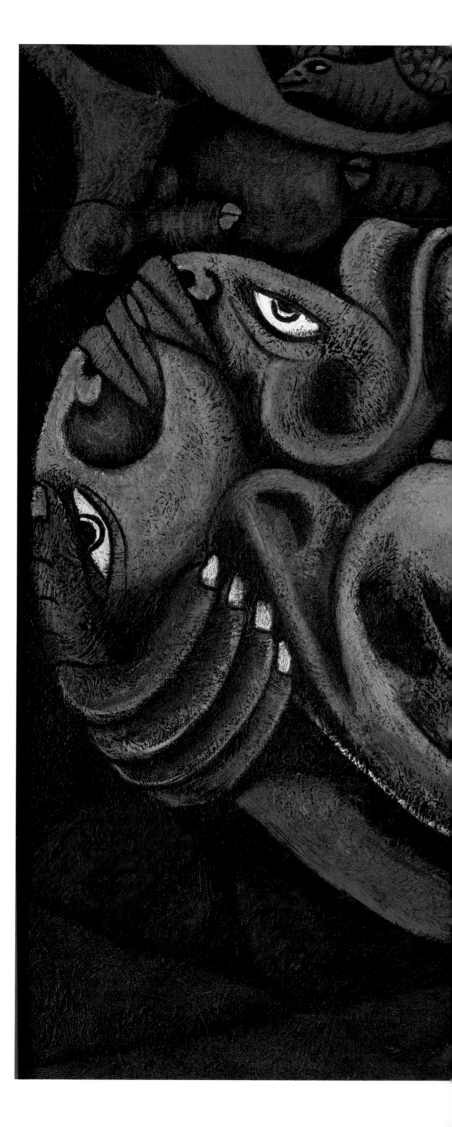

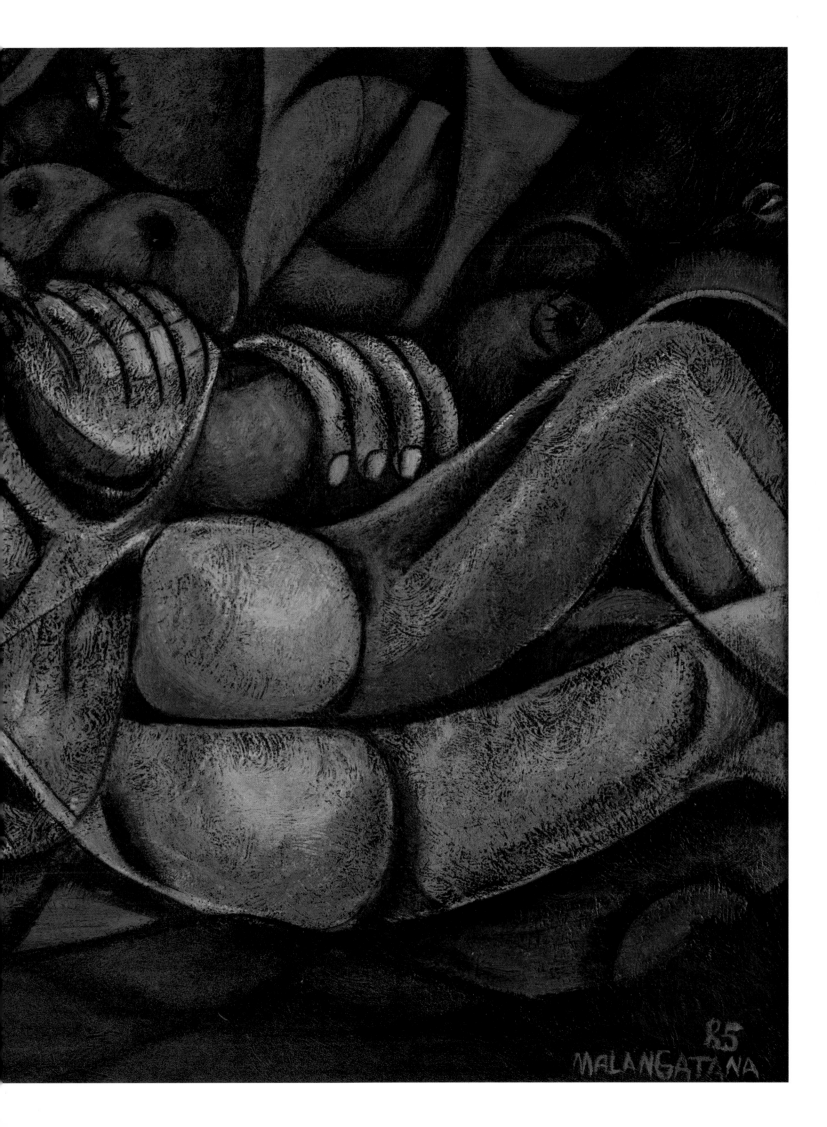

O Poço Sagrado
The Sacred Well

1985

Onde Está a Minha Mãe, os Meus Irmãos e Todos os Outros?
Where Are My Mother, My Brothers, and All the Others?
1986

I *II*

Como Amar um Amado Há Tantos Anos?
How To Love a Loved One After So Many Years?

1986

O Meu Poema
My Poem
1987

154

Sem título
Untitled

1987

Sonho

Dream

1987-1988

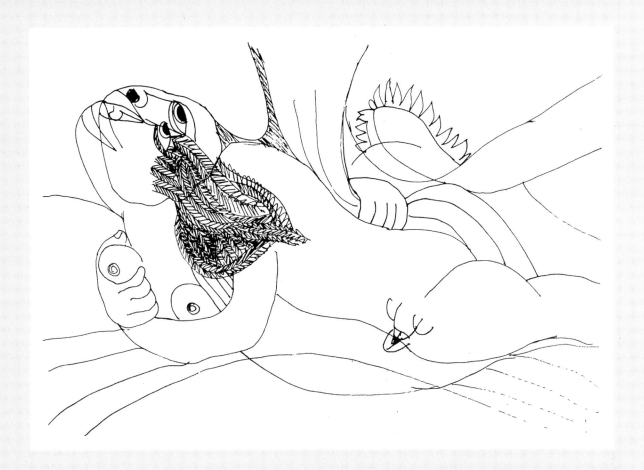

Amor
Love

1988

Retrato da Gelita em Silêncio
Portrait of Gelita in Silence

1988

Sem título
Untitled

1988

Homenagem a Hloyasi
(a minha mãe)
Homage to Hloyasi
(my mother)

1988

Sem título
Untitled

1989

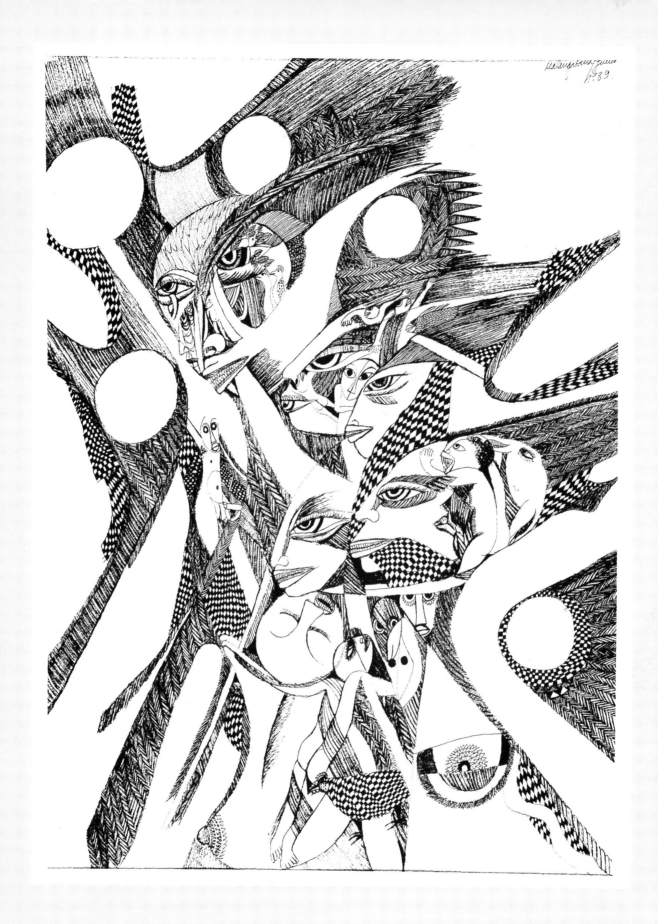

Finjo Que não Choro/e/quando as Lágrimas Caem/Digo com Olhos Sorrindo/à Elefanta/
/Que tudo Vai no melhor Caminho
I pretend that I do not cry/and/When the tears fall/I say with my eyes smiling/to the sow elephant/
/That everything is on the best track

1989

O Olhar Erótico
The Erotic Glance

1989

Baila Meu Corpo/Escuta a Música de Ti-Próprio
Dance, my body/Listen to your inner music

1990

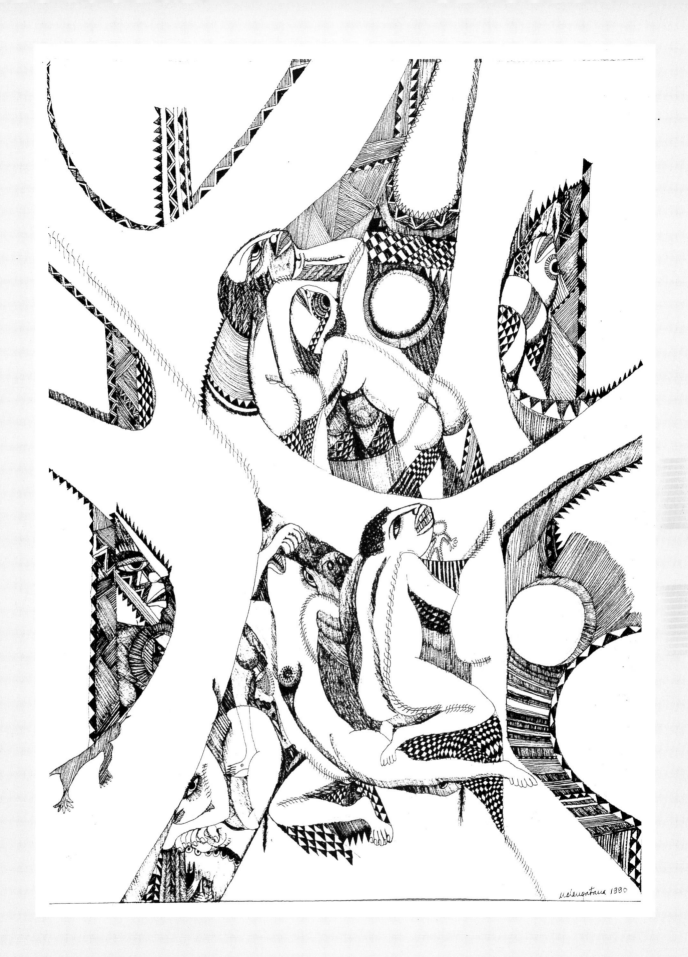

Os Emaranhados
The Entangled

1990

165

Eros Incubando o Amor
Eros Incubating Love

1991

Ritos
Rituals

1991

Transparências
Transparencies
1991

Canção ao Sol
Song to the Sun

1992

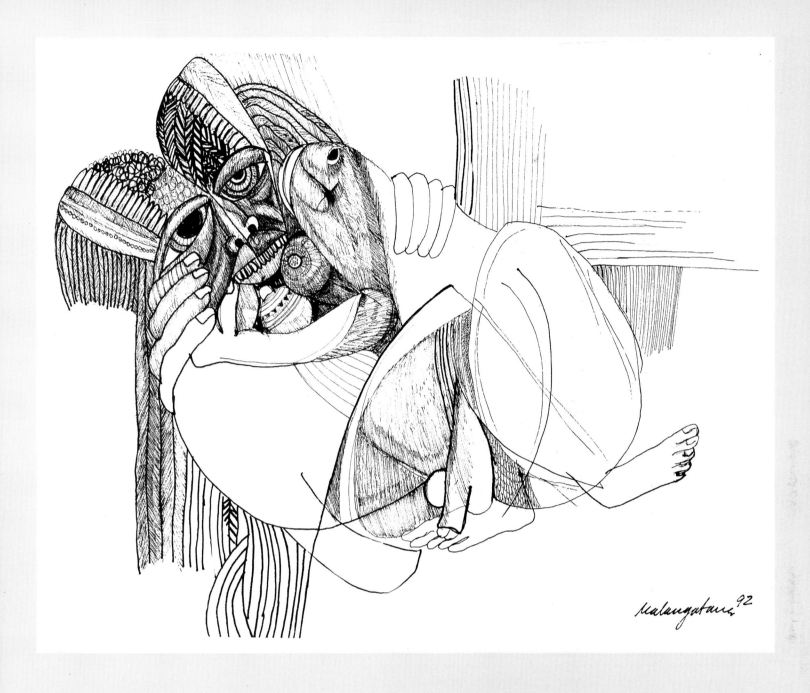

Quando a Deusa Quer mais
<u>*When the Goddess Wants More*</u>

1992

Relatos do Tempo da Guerra dos 15 Anos
Accounts of the Fifteen-Year War
1992

Sem título
Untitled
Africa Pavilion, Expo '92, Seville

1992

O Voo das Pombas Sagradas
The Flight of the Sacred Doves
1993

O Menino Verde
The Green Boy

1993

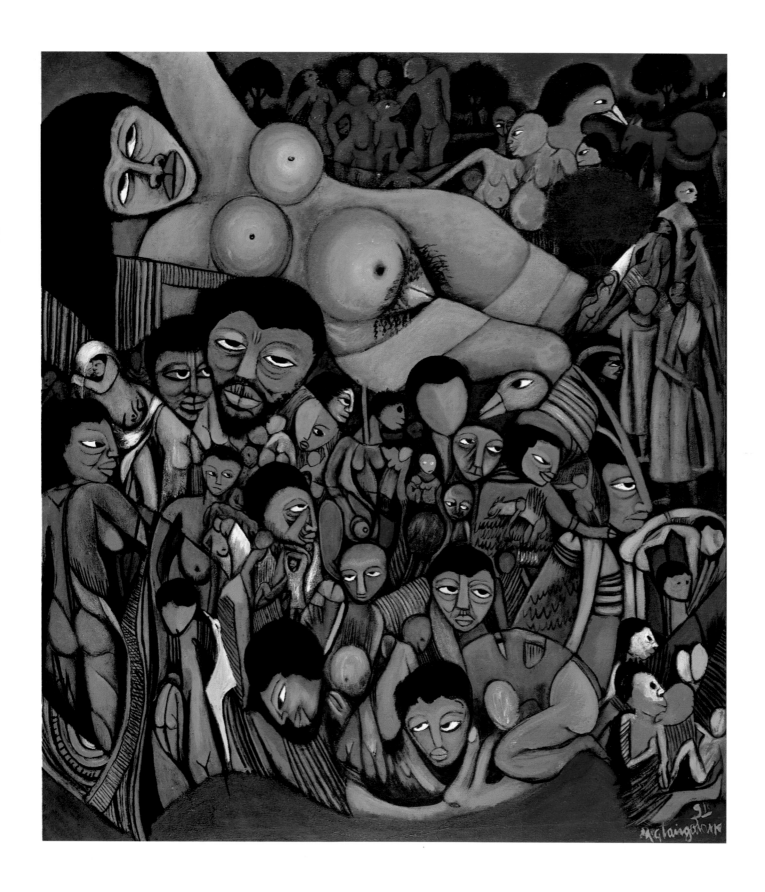

Os Exaustos
The Exhausted Ones

1994

Sinais
Signals

1994

Ambilu ya ngwenya ye tondôôô
The Heart of the Crocodile is at Peace

1994

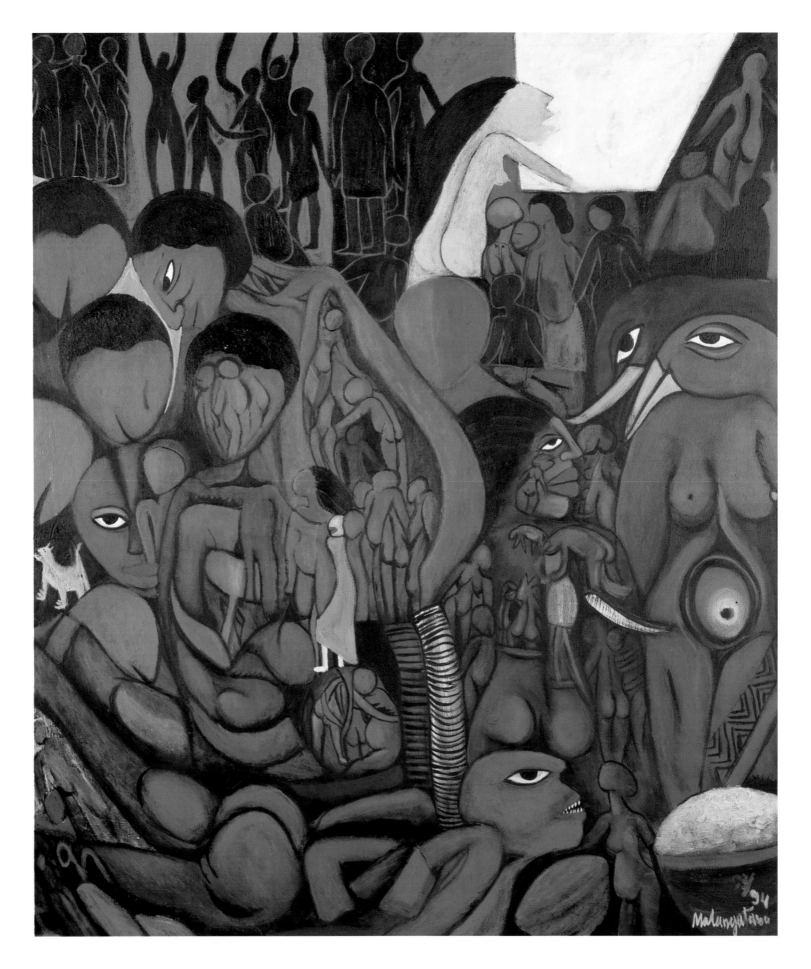

A Mulher Que Vai ao Espelho e não Vê a Sua Cara
The Woman Who Stands before the Mirror and Does not See her Face

1994

Já Votei
I Have Already Voted

1994

Escultura

Sculpture

1995

Até o Menino Voltou
Even the Boy Returned

1995

Ritual Nocturno
Nocturnal Ritual ▶

1995

188

Primavera Radiosa
Radiant Spring

1995

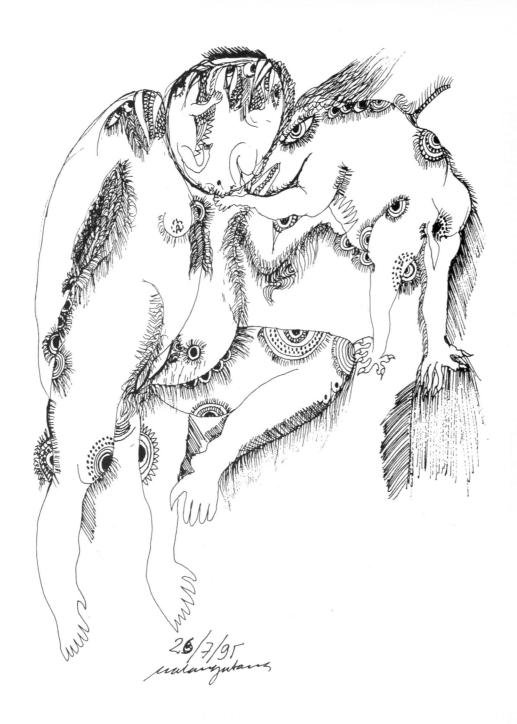

26/7/95

Sem título
Untitled

1995

39/99   Emergir I   Malangatana 96

Emergir I
Emerging I

1996

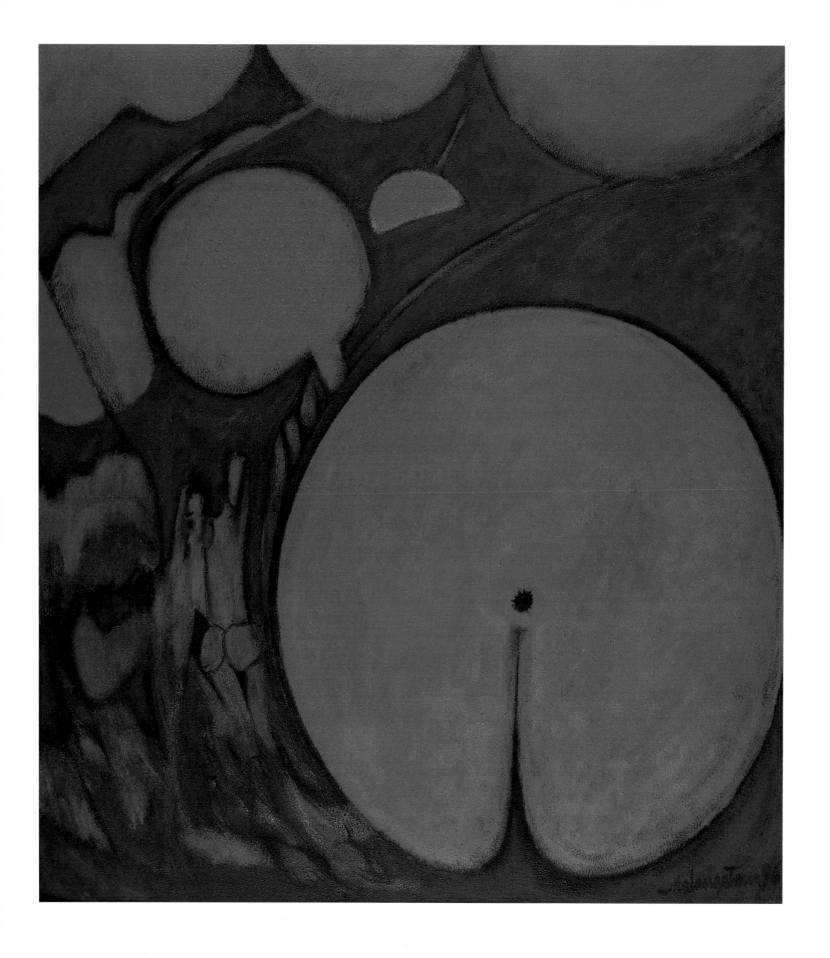

Olhar Permanente
The Permanent Gaze

1996

Estou Aterrorizado com as Queimadas
I Am Terrified by the Burnings

1996

Sem título
Untitled
1998

Sem título
Untitled
1998

About Malangatana

Este quadros são o resultado de pouco mais de um ano e meio de trabalho de um ex-criado de bar.

Malangatana é um pintor natural, completo. Nele a composição, a harmonia de cores, não é jogo intelectual; acontece-lhe, tão naturalmente como as histórias e as visões.

Ele sabe sem saber.

A sua visão tem estranhos paralelos com a tradição europeia. Certos quadros aproximam-se dos primitivos catalães, outros das aparições macabras dos visionários holandeses e ainda outros são de um surrealismo involuntário, directo e mágico.

Ele aparenta derivar dessa tradição mas sem jamais ter tido acesso a ela e sem qualquer ensinamento.

Ele é visitado por espíritos; certos quadros são alucinações, fragmentos de um inferno que já foi de Bosch.

Malangatana tem um conhecimento profundo das razões subterrâneas dos homens, o que aliado à sua extraordinária visão formal produz pintura de uma totalidade tão rara que apesar de ele ser um principiante já é um dos primeiros pintores de África.

Amâncio d'Alpoim Guedes
Catalogue for his first solo exhibit, April 1961

Bertina: Mesmo que residamos tu na Polana, o Malangatana para lá de Mavalane e eu na Munhuana um elo indestrutível liga-nos. O elo é como somos porque assim nascemos. [...]

Há uma sobrecarga psicológica em nós. Um permanente turbilhão de sensações.

Rejeitar uma cultura regionalista é negarmonos. Os que não sentem a mesma motivação é porque são Gloriosos, Imanentes e transferem para o plano da supremacia técnica também o seu sentido do Belo. São Perfeitos. Cultura para esses está para além do lugar. Porque se transcontinentalizam e já não vivem a intensidade do lar-terra como uma verdade cósmica. Libertaram-se. Emigraram. Não experimentam a nostalgia do clã se não por um esforço da inteligência e não do emocional. Não vivem o circunstancial. [...]

É absurdo admitir que vivendo todos a mesma época reagimos da mesma maneira. O substrato interior tem fases. Nuns ultrapassou, noutros estagnou e noutros tende a uma reimpenetração. O teu caso, o meu, o do Malangatana e o da reimpenetração de que saímos redimidos. [...]

Para nós Arte é também a reivindicação da nossa identidade no mundo dos homens. A linguagem em que pedimos que nos aceitem, nos amem e nos respeitem. E se estamos errados a culpa não é tua nem minha.

Acabou-se, Bertina. É tudo.

José Craveirinha
In the newspaper *Notícias*, Lourenço Marques, in the 1960s

[...] The canvases of Valente Malangatana of Mozambique also bear the mark of history, history in conflict with crushing social pressure, with foreign definitions of moral and immoral, of God and the Devil. His fantastic scenes crammed with the bulky forms of powerful demons and vuloptuous women are contemporary mythology in the same sense as the attenuated images of Ibrahim el Salahi. [...]

Ulli Beier
Contempory African Art, 1ª edition, England, 1962

[...] It is to be hoped that experience and maturity will lead him to a greater respect for the physical properties of his pointings; his astonishing energy, however, leaves no doubt that here is a pioneer of the New Africa unafraid to exploit his vision and heritage to the fullest.

Dennis Williams
Wedwardy, August 15, 1962

[...] Os meus temas principais são: ódio, feitiço, crime, angústia, paixão pela vida e amor. Estes temas não estão só na pintura mas também na poesia. Tudo isto sinto no coração e quando faço qualquer trabalho sem sentir; nunca sou eu o autor desse trabalho, o que me leva então a estar a fazer outra coisa quando o sentimento me falta. [...]

Malangatana Valente
«Malangatana Valente tells the story of the painting which won the prize for painting", in *Voz Africana*, September 15, 1962

This exciting artist is only twenty six years old and has now been painting for about three years. [...]

Malangatana's work is wild and powerful, but it is more than that: far from being repelled by the scenes of horror, we are brought under an irresistible spell. For Malangatana's work also contains a strong element of human sympathy and suffering and agony. Malangatana is anxious to communicate through his paintings. He is full of stories. Sometimes one picture is not enough to tell the whole story and so he has to paint a series with a sequence. Sometimes he has to use words in addition to images and he scribbles his message on the canvas.

Malangatana is one of the few really original painters to be found in Africa today. Considering the fact that he has been handling oilpaints for only three years, his technical achievement is also remarkable.

This is his first one man show outside Lourenço Marques. But undoubtedly the world will hear more about this gifted artist.

Ulli Beier
1962

[...] Malangatana Ngwenya Valente é quase um fenómeno de floração espontânea e de prodigiosa adivinhação. A sua arte, que radica num sentimento poético da vida, define-se pelo emblemático, pelo mágico, pelo onírico. Desde as visões de um Buda negro às suas apetências simbolizadas — como na Viagem interior, nitidamente tangencial ao surrealismo, ele nos comunica o seu mundo de vivências com uma intensidade de coloridos crus quase ofuscante e um labiríntico senso de composição, em que o ritmo pessoalíssimo, por completo à solta, destrói os arranjos convencionais de perspectiva. Pintor da carne, do desejo, do medo, do sagrado. Malangatana traz para a sua pintura híbrida de africanismo e lusitanidade com inflitrações católicas e sugestões já literárias do humanismo europeu — o poder do riso e o furor do sexo. [...]

"Two Mozambican painters: Malangatana and Muchanga", *Jornal de Artes e Letras*, April 17, 1963

[...] Ele faz parte de uma geração de artistas que começaram uma tradição enchendo o vazio existente entre o antigo e o novo, campo e cidade, cultura. Quando Malangatana pinta médicos-curandeiros com cruzes cristãs ao pescoço ou africanos com cabelos compridos ele mostra talvez que esses fossos não são tão profundos para não poderem ser preenchidos e que o valor de uma obra de arte é o de mostrar qualidades universais, mais que particularidades específicas de pequenos grupos.

Julian Beinart
Education of Vision/Gyor Gy Repes. Brussels: La Connaissance, 1967

Dele, disse Afonso Cautela: "Do pintor Malangatana irrompe um mundo brutal que a arte da sensibilidade inigualável deste filho de Matalana adoça, sublima e purifica. Uma fauna de híbridos seres, uma flora inexpugnável, um universo onde se conjugam as forças desencadeadas da magia negra e as forças boas, curativas, benéficas, da magia branca. Sabe-se hoje, depois de os surrealistas a terem pesquisado, que a arte fantástica se liga a uma experiência de fundo mágico — e Malangatana, sem saber nem querer saber nada de surrealismo, percorre essa via do realismo fantástico com a segurança e a ferocidade de quem 'sabe' muito [...]

"Malangatana copied. Discussion of a falsification", *Século Illustrado*, December 1972

[...] As he writes in his autobiography, "[...] poetry is art written on white paper without color and in repeated letters, but poetry in a picture has life, smell and movement also [...]" For him, poetry is painting in words, art in words.

[...] Malangatana feels that any art which fails to express the anxieties and aspirations of the people is insignificant. He "feels sad" when a style of art does not communicate with the spectator: "[...] a simple dialogue, comprehensible, but having all the requirements of art. A vibrant thing, crying to the spectator, full of heat and life that makes him cry, or creates in his body. Thus, it's worthwhile to have art, to make it, to express it as a force of our veins and with the heat of our blood. It ought to be executed with the same passion in which lovers enter in that subconscious relationship at the exact moment of possession. In this manner we look at a statue, a painting, or we read a poem, as if hearing a guitar or a *Nitende* whose metal wires were forged in the ardent fire burning for centuries in the hearts of the people." [...]

Betty Schneider
"Malangatana, Mozambique", in *African Arts*, 1972, UCLA

[...] Assim, atento à poética transmitida nos contos populares do seu povo, não esquecendo no tratamento da figura humana as lições da sua escultura, representando mesmo certos motivos decorativos da sua cerâmica e do seu artesanato, Malangatana quase nada fica a dever à pintura ocidental. A presença da cultura «branca» está todavia presente nesta arte fantástica, em evocações de carácter literário ou religioso, presença contraditória e por vezes absurda, a determinar talvez o clima trágico de certas visões. Pintor sem «escola», elemento solitário num cruzamento cultural muito particular, desconhecendo as academias e pintando como sabe, Malangatana tem o instinto e a força de um autêntico «ingénuo», obrigado a elaborar sozinho a sua linguagem e o seu canto. [...]

[...] Mas em Malangatana a consciência da realidade é sofrida até ao mais profundo do ser e é por isso que ela se entrelaça e confunde com os sonhos e desejos do inconsciente, é por isso que ela se faz grito, vivência funda, realidade vivida. A pintura de Malangatana nada tem de exercício académico, é precisamente o contrário disso e o seu autor seria certamente chumbado em todas as academias.

A consciência do pintor identifica-se com os sofrimentos e com a alma de um povo, a sua pintura chega a ganhar a voz de uma raça. Em quantos artistas do neo-realismo aconteceu semelhante processo de identificação?

Francisco Bronze
In the magazine *Colóquio*, Lisbon, 1973

Clara ou obscura, programada ou instintiva, completa ou balbuciante, a pintura de Malangatana procura talvez fixar o que durante a noite o faz acordar e o que durante o dia o faz pensar no que sonhou: um quotidiano de fome, de humilhação, de raiva, de terror, de violência, de ternura, de cio, de desespero e de esperança. [...]

[...] Enquanto na Europa se vê que os ditames da revolução social continuam a atender apenas à dimensão pragmática da expressão, querendo calar o sujeito, vemos os novos mundos pegar nas chamadas velhas linguagens europeias e torná-las revolucionárias precisamente através de uma forte subjectivização. Mas talvez se venha a perceber um dia que a arte válida europeia dos nossos dias continuou a ser feita por excepções, e que os mais revolucionários são os mais românticos. [...]

[...] Entre os citados pólos deste ingénuo realismo fantástico africano — e ingénuo porque sabiamente não quer esquecer o que só ele pode fazer lembrar — há quadros em que se incluem sinais das artes decorativas locais, onde há síntese de grafismo de ordem individual e de ordem colectiva. Falando de si, Malangatana fala dos seus semelhantes e para aqueles que se identificam, se descobrem seus semelhantes.

Rui Mário Gonçalves
Preface to solo exhibition, Bucholz, Lisbon, 1973

Partindo de um expressionismo visceral, enraizadamente africano, a pintura de Malangatana atinge o fantástico e o visionário. A sua imaginação libérrima manifesta um mundo telúrico cheio de sol e aspereza, onde os homens sofrem e vivem os mesmos anseios, sonham e encontram uma ordem biológica no caos da aflição e do drama; gente corajosa que grita e olha de frente, que conhece o amor e a crueldade, sobretudo a crueldade das suas próprias visões alucinatórias, autênticos pesadelos que não deixam dormir e que tão profundamente motivam e marcam a pintura de Malangatana. [...]

[...] A pintura de Malangatana é a revelação desse drama comum: um mundo de pavor e sangue, de desespero e insegurança, de amor e agressividade, de exotismo e erotismo, em que tudo se humaniza num ritual de fome e sexo, em que animais de forma fálica como lagartos viscosos e rastejantes, com dentes, garras e cicatrizes, invadem quase totalmente o espaço da tela. [...]

[...] Pintor temperamentalmente avesso à integração em qualquer escola, Malangatana tem o instinto e a força de um autêntico «ingénuo» que pinta como só ele sabe e não como porventura lhe pretendam ensinar. Imensamente mais atento à sua voz interior, que é também a de todos aqueles que consigo se identificam, como ontem, hoje, afirmo, reafirmo que Malangatana como pintor e homem incarna a alma africana na sua pujança magnífica de ardor, pureza, desejo e ritmo.

Eurico Gonçalves
"Malangatana, the fantastic expressionism of a popular painter", in the supplement to *A República*, July 26, 1973

[...] Malangatana Ngwenya du Mozambique a consacré ses dessins typiques aux événements de Soweto. Lorsque sa patrie était encore une colonie portugaise, il avait créé une série de dessins et de peintures provocatrices disséquant les contrastes de la société. Ses oeuvres étaient peuplés de personnages menacés par les griffes de monstres aux dents énormes; les chaînes n'apparaîssaient pas seulement aux mains et aux jambes. Malangatana Ngwenya a participé en tant que délégué du Mozambique libre et progressiste à l'Assemblée mondiale pour la paix et la vie, contre la guerre nucléaire, tenue cette année à Prague. Dans sa patrie indépendante, il appartient au nombre des artistes éminents, et ses fresques ornent les plus importants édifices publics. Il organise des expositions des peintres et sculpteurs mozambicains contemporains, contribue à la formation des jeunes artistes. Malangatana a écrit dans un mémoire, le 25 juin 1983 dans la capitale tchécoslovaque, Prague: "A Prague, pendant l'Assemblée mondiale pour la paix, j'ai vécu chaque instant por un avenir meilleur."

Alvis Wottoun
"Social Mission of the New African Art", *Culture en Solidarité*, 1983

La pintura de Malangatana no termina en el lienzo. Según la tradición africana, el artista no heredó sólo un saber, sino que fue, investido de capacidades mágicas, por lo que se convierte en un médium, un mensajero del mundo de las sombras y los espiritus… De una exposición de Malangatana se sale con la sensación de que ya no somos los mismos que cuando entramos… La tensión creada en el lienzo no permite que permanezcamos confinados en él, obliga a buscar un orden exterior al cuadro. Aquí reside finalmente el genio refinado de este «ingenuo» invocador del caos, sabio perturbador de nuestra certidumbre…

Cusa
In *Cartelera*, November 27, 1984

Na tradição africana, o fantástico, o mundo povoado de animais astutos e também monstros horrendos e onde ocorrem as situações inquietantes mais insólitas, transmissível e enriquecido historicamente, é escola de valores e forma de desenvolver capacidades intelectuais e criativas das crianças.

Cosmogonia que se insere na cultura popular, o imaginário é evocado normalmente à noite, à volta da fogueira, rearticulando o verosímil e o inverosímil, o verdadeiro e o falso e fazendo surgir situações antes tidas por impossíveis, numa dialéctica que não explica o mundo, mas procura imbuir a sociedade de respeito pelas normas que garantem a estrutura dessa sociedade e pelos valores culturais que lhe são próprios.

Com o ritual mágico do gesto e da palavra, o conto, a narração, a canção e o passo de dança, magnetiza-se a assistência e estimulam-se as crianças, fazendo revelar as mais dotadas de memória e vivacidade. Com a curiosidade infinita da infância, Malangatana bebeu avidamente a água de todos os sabores deste rio de seiva do seu povo.

Vivendo uma relação, permanente e enriquecedora, com este universo de valores, Malangatana é hoje um narrador de histórias do imaginário popular que ultrapassou o quadro étnico original e integrou no seu sistema símbolos, códigos e signos do património universal, que inserem a trajectória da sua obra na nova cultura que une a humanidade nesta segunda metade do século vinte.

[…] A vida de Malangatana ocorre num período de profundas alterações sociais, que procuram desarticular o sistema de valores tradicional, em que o processo de despersonalização cultural provocado pelo colonial-fascismo se fazia impor com particular violência, para que se adoptassem simplesmente os valores ocidentais através da assimilação cultural iniciada há muito.

A sua obra tem por isso a força de uma cultura longamente oprimida, que se liberta com violência até se impor com a sua identidade própria. Falar de Malangatana é falar de Moçambique, de África, dos seus mistérios, da sua libertação, do seu quotidiano de preocupações.

"Malangatana, Mozambican Painter", text inserted in catalogue for his retrospective, Maputo, 1986

[…] Desse modo temos o período de 1959 a 1961, período que reúne as primeiras obras do artista até à sua primeira exposição individual. De 1961 a 1964, entre a sua primeira "individual" e a sua prisão pela PIDE. 1964 e 1965, o seu tempo nas celas da PIDE. Da sua saída da cadeia (1965) até à primeira saída do país e ida à Europa (1971). A sua estada em Lisboa e noutras localidades da Europa (1971-1973). 1973 e 1974 é a passagem pela Suíça e pós-Europa. Depois, de 1974 a 1978, é a Pré-Independência, a Independência, até à sua partida para o trabalho junto das Aldeias Comunais na província de Nampula. Aí permanece até 1980 e nova "maneira" também surge. Depois de 1980 é o Malangatana de hoje.

Júlio Navarro
"The Various Phases of Malangatana's Work (1)", in the weekly magazine *Tempo*, May 4, 1986

[…] Estes rostos repetidos até à exaustão do espaço, estas figuras torcidas por uma infinita amargura não são imagens deste mundo criado por nós e, afinal, contra nós. Monstros que julgávamos há muito extintos dentro de nós são ressuscitados no pincel de Malangatana. Ressurge um temor que nos atemoriza porque é o nosso velho desadormecido. Ficamos assim à mercê destas visões, somos assaltados pela fragilidade da nossa representação visual do Universo.

Este salto do tradicional para o moderno foi feito sem pedir ajuda à assimilação colonial. Malangatana atravessou incólume todo o convívio com um ambiente que convidava à despersonalização. O seu fito era recolher técnicas que concedessem melhor expressão aos seus pincéis. No seu traço está nua e tangível a geografia do tempo africano. No jogo das cores está, cruel e sedutor, o feitiço.

O crescer das suas capacidades fez-se sem que houvesse deslize para um outro terreno, forte nas raízes que criaram com a sua terra e o seu tempo.

A pintura de Malangatana não termina na tela: prossegue trabalhando dentro de nós. De acordo com a tradição africana, o artista não herdou apenas um saber mas foi investido com capacidades mágicas tornando-se um médium, um mensageiro do mundo das sombras e dos espíritos.

Sai-se de uma exposição de Malangatana com a sensação de que já não somos os mesmos que éramos quando entrámos. As visões monstruosas que ele partilhou connosco nesse curto espaço de tempo fizeram-nos cúmplices dos corpos esquartejados, do sangue escorrendo com ternura além do vermelho. Afinal, fomos também esses ternos assassinos da arrumação natural do mundo, violamos a ordem das cores e dos contornos, redesenhamos com ele as linhas do Universo.

Estes olhos que se acumulam na superfície do papel espreitam-nos com intenção maliciosa. Somos vistos pelo quadro, o pintor visita o nosso interior surpreendendo-nos na incapacidade de o vermos como ele nos vê a nós.

Estes bichos e homens atirados para um espaço

tornado exíguo pelo acumular de elementos gráficos procuram em nós uma saída. A tensão criada na tela não permite que fiquem confinados a ela, obriga-os a procurar uma ordem exterior ao quadro. Aqui reside afinal o génio apurado deste "ingénuo" invocador do caos, sábio perturbador das nossas certezas.

Mia Couto
"The ingenuous genius", in the Cultural Supplement of *O Diário*, August 24, 1986

Malangatana, amigo — tivemos ambos a felicidade de ter vivido uma revelação mútua. Em ti, vimos que a África encontrou o caminho independente para a expressão própria e forte na sua pintura. Tu viste em nós a compreensão, a estima e a amizade para com o vosso povo. Estamos gratos pelo encontro que nos uniu humanamente.

Margot Dias
May, 1986

[...] Una pittura densa, piena, con colori violenti e caldi, senza spazi liberi in un continuo intrecciarsi di forme, ricca di simbolismi e di citazioni popolari, o semplicemente di vita, da leggersi come si potrebbe leggere un quadro di Bosch o, non fraintendetemi, un pannello dei nostri cantastorie del Sud Italia.

Parallelamente alla sua instancabile attività pittorica, e soprattuto per meglio definire la sua figura di artista "totale", e di personaggio, sono da ricordarsi le sue opere scultoree in ferro, le ceramiche, le sue capacità sonore e vocali, e non ultimi i suoi poemi e poesie.

Da alcuni anni da'il suo notevole appoggio alla Segreteria di Stato della Cultura, aiutando e stimolando il lavoro dei giovani artisti mozambicani.

Gin Angri
Maputo, August 1986

At this point I would like to continue with a few more remarks from the interview, covering mainly those aspects which relate to Malangatana's involvement in the "little school", and the relationship between his work and that of the children.

"We are not just trying to teach the children one thing, we are trying to give them another life, and with this we started to see something very important: in this area there are some primary and secondary schools. The children themselves have started to exert a big influence in the school. Some of the teachers to see the changes, as a few of the children began to advise the teachers as to what they should do when they dont have water paints, paper or coloured pencils. Then these teachers came to the 'escolinha vamos brincar' to see what we were doing, and we now have

quite a good link with the schools. The 'school' is now starting to spread to other zones.

"What is important for me about the learning group is that it also forces me to go back to my roots. It makes me start from the beginning and helps me see where I came from."

"Through the children so much has been influenced in my life now. My letters are changing, and I see that I have developed a different way of thinking, as a result of discussing with the children."

"They have made me think more about my art, and the colours I use. I use colours now that I was not using before, like brownish colours and strong black colours."

"The 'escolinha' is still acquiring new children, today for instance I saw some children whom I have never seen before, and that is good, because they bring some beautiful drawings. Of course, these newcomers are often aldready influenced by the more regular children."

"What is very important is that the 'escolinha' is not working only in the square of sand that you have seen, but now if you walk around this area you will see children doing the same things as they are accustomed to doing in the 'escolinha' and this is very important, because this shows that they don't need to come on Sunday only, in order to have something to do, and to develop themselves."

Meira Visser
"Little School Let's Play: The Children as Artists and the Artist as a Child" in *Wateford Kamhlaba U.W.C.*, 1986

"No princípio, foi a confusão: principalmente depois da minha primeira exposição individual, na então Lourenço Marques, as pessoas falavam de mim, da minha pintura, das cores que eu usava, do meu traço, e eu, não as compreendia. Diziam-me surrealista ou naïf, chamavam os meus temas de fantasmagóricos, referiam coisas como o inconsciente colectivo, procuravam referências comparativas em Gauguin ou Bosch: eu não as entendia. Depois, no estrangeiro, na Cidade do Cabo, em Paris, na Checoslováquia, na Índia, sobretudo na Nigéria, onde os meus quadros ou as suas fotografias são mostrados a partir de 1961, falam dos dadaístas como ponto de referência obrigatória para a minha pintura, do movimento Bauhaus — mas tudo isto me confunde, eu não sabia o que tudo isso significava nem qual o seu interesse.

"Por isso procurei saber o que as pessoas queriam efectivamente dizer-me, procurei conhecer o significado de todos esses nomes e de todos esses termos, através de leituras, do estudo da história da pintura e da arquitectura, de contactos com amigos, fazendo perguntas. Hoje, em parte, eu já ultrapassei essa fase de atrapalhação, de ignorância sobre o que diziam da minha pintura, sobre esses temas e essas comparações aplicadas à minha obra. E, sem dúvida, reencontrei-me em algumas delas.

"Este foi um processo difícil e que levou muito tempo mas que me permitiu adquirir conhecimentos técnicos e gerais sobre a arte que se reflectiram positivamente sobre a pintura que fazia e sobre a minha sensibilidade como pintor.

"A minha infância não foi nem alegre nem triste. Mas eu vivi a situação colonial a ver os meus pais, a minha família, muita gente que eu conhecia a ir para o trabalho forçado, a ser obrigada a seguir para as minas no estrangeiro para poder viver, e isso marcou-me profundamente. No entanto, quando comecei a pintar, não foram esses os temas que fui buscar em primeiro lugar: isso foi apenas mais tarde. O que inicialmente eu procuro reproduzir são temas relacionados com as histórias que eu ouvira contar aos anciãos, são temas sobre a mitologia e sobre o curandeirismo, sobre o passado e sobre o presente da terra onde eu nascera, temas com os quais eu, felizmente, me identificava. Ora esses temas não são nem alegres nem tristes: as cores aparecem abertas e claras, não há cinzentos nessa altura na minha pintura. Só mais tarde, com o desenvolvimento de uma consciência política, as situações de dor, a denúncia do colonialismo, passam a ser uma constante na minha pintura. Não há alegria nela, mas há este relacionamento constante com a realidade que eu vivi. Hoje, de certo modo, esta característica mantém-se. Mas a verdade é que a guerra e a dor continuam presentes: é difícil e sangrento este nascer do mundo novo no nosso País.

"Seja como for, não são estes os únicos temas na minha pintura. Nunca deixei de pintar o amor, as brincadeiras, naturezas-mortas. Tal como hoje nesta terra massacrada, e apesar da guerra, há uma grande dinâmica de reconstrução nacional, uma grande dinâmica política e social, a agricultura reassume uma força explosiva, os camiões continuam a circular, as pessoas viajam pelo mar, pelas estradas e caminhos, pelo mato, apesar da guerra e da destruição. Ora isto reflecte-se, necessariamente, na minha arte, esta é também uma forma de contribuir para erguer este país a níveis cada vez mais altos."

Jorge Costa
"Malangatana Ngwenya: yesterday, today, and tomorrow", in *Revista Índico*, no. 3, 1989

Malangatana's drawing

[...]

Temos ocasião assim de poder apreciar as suas composições de *papel cheio* em que os sinais de um barroquismo sempre fortemente integrado, emanescente do tradicional vêm marcar as suas principais preocupações: o seu Povo, a sua Terra, o Amor, a Vida, em suma, as preocupações naturais de uma grande força telúrica como Malangatana é. Mas a estas, detalhadas e surpreendentes de achados em todos os pequenos espaços, vêm-se juntar aquelas de um traço despojado, em que os brancos vêm fazer viver as figuras, emprestar-lhes o movimento de que elas respiram. Ou ainda a ligação destas duas maneiras num conjugar enriquecedor do despojamento do traço, reduzido ao essencial, e um envoltório barroco, fremente de sinais, bichos e gentes. Também aqui podemos encontrar quando, como em "O regresso dos cadáveres em Angola", o tema é por de mais dramático para se casar com uma rebuscada elaboração, e surge um desenho quase *sujo*, bruto, aparentemente inacabado, mas onde é a emoção de momento, imediata, que brota em cachão, e o realiza.

Utilizando o preto como cor normal no desenho, Malangatana faz, no entanto, algumas incursões na cor, quase sempre uma só cor — na maior parte das vezes os castanhos-terra —, muito raramente, como em *Homenagem a Hloyasi*, com mais. Parece sentir-se que o Artista sente a cor — e como sabemos que a sente e domina bem — essencialmente como Pintura. No Desenho, ela surge só quando uma proposta que o apaixona não lhe deixa outra solução.

O Desenho para ele — e parece não haver dúvidas de que bem o prova — é a riqueza do traço capaz de dar corpo a toda a imensa imaginação e criatividade que consegue expandir através dos mais intrincados rebuscamentos ou do traço mais limpo, as suas profundas emoções, o seu sentir profundamente moçambicano, africano e de habitante por inteiro da totalidade deste nosso planeta Terra.

The Friends of the National Museum of Art, in the *National Museum of Art* exhibit catalogue, Maputo, 1993

O meu fascínio pela pintura de Malangatana peca por mágica ingenuidade É assim que acordo de noite assaltada por extractos ciclópicos do seu discurso surreal Confundo-os com pedaços soltos de um sonho ou desejo embalado nos braços que a mente acaricia Ao pensamento afluem-me ideias que jamais tive e deixo-me desafiar pela brancura do papel As palavras vão soltar-se como contas de rosário nas mãos ainda abertas de medo O crucifixo cristão no pescoço de um negro africano perturba-me Inquietam-me os seus longos lisos cabelos Os vermelhos e a tinta a escorrer como sangue Os fantasmas dos corpos disformes As armas flores pássaros e algemas Os monstros e as delícias Os falos A irreal transcendência a deslumbrar o escuro A magia negra e a magia branca interagindo obrigando os seres aos seus oníricos percursos Um olho visionário a determinar os acontecimentos Milhares de espaços intermináveis fixam-se nos olhos de quem espreita Nas bocas cerradas Não merece a pena estancar o apocalipse A fuga é centrífuga Só resta o panelão ao fogo Os polvos familiares ritualizando o amor e a guerra Através das máscaras de dentes aguçados Haverá sempre denúncias Um mocho atentíssimo a qualquer movimento que adultere feitiços Persistirá o mistério da partilha dos sinais que o inconsciente teima em não explicar A não ser pela empatia plena que fez do capturado captor e vice-versa Excessivo o jogo da paixão Que é pura luz a derramar-se pela extrema melancolia Dos olhares que observam a fome de tudo Excepto da dor e da sensualidade Estranha sedução a que perdura no outro em todos os outros Conquistando fantasias e acrescentando-as Com um saber inteiro de perturbante caçador de espíritos Ele o pintor arrebata-nos para o seu caos de aflição misteriosa Mensageiro do drama apanha-nos desprevenidos de poderes criativos Irmana-nos no encantamento das fontes do sagrado esquecidos da violência Atira-me mansamente para abismos insondáveis associados às benéficas forças naturais Numa cumplicidade de silêncios e de olhares a moerem enigmas Lembra "atrevidamente" a existência fálica de bichos e homens que buscam saídas através dos nossos pactos de invasores Exprime-se por imagens com o gozo dos deuses mas é dentro da alma que arquiva a imensidão africana do coração dos homens Na estridência aflitiva dum silêncio que transcende os sentimentos que desperta No entanto procuro explicações, para o acto mágico de ele trabalhar a sensualidade dos outros espreitando cruamente para o seu interior.

Aconteceu naquele primeiríssimo contacto nosso na sua casa-*atelier* em Maputo Chuva cósmica ofuscando os meus espantos Assimilando o caos ordenado duma vida-toda-tantos-quadros Muitos pontos de luz e sangue chamaram os meus sentidos que a um só tempo se abriam e cerravam O criador genuíno penetrou então a minha alma sem a invadir quando a sua presença física ainda não estava visível Formaram-se imagens na minha cabeça a percepcionar o seu fantástico realismo Que eu (re)conhecia vagamente de há muito tempo antes sem contudo atentar na exacta realização do contorno e da mancha desta pintura O seu traço Suas formas seu enxameado espaço Sua luz estridente Suas cores Sua harmonia e sequência progressiva ingénua rude ou mais soberba na sua multiplicidade sempre a infiltrar-se na água espessa da minha atenção Pela poesia emanente do discurso pictório Foi então que ele apareceu e me guiou em profundo silêncio vigiando-me Uma espécie de identificação de instintos células ou raízes nasceu entre nós Nesse complexo de quadros saturando as paredes das salas se contam mil e uma histórias exóticas e eróticas Reais e inventadas De fábula onde os bichos se acariciam com línguas pontiagudas e os corpos se recontorcem de volúpia Revelando personagens cheios de cio raiva e ternura Contam histórias em linguagem que o fantástico descodifica Para se prenderem à flor de leituras íntimas seguindo rumos inimagináveis Um discurso onírico pleno de ritmo transmite o vigor da memória ancestral dum povo que se reconhece pelos signos valores e ritos A alquimia operada redunda na explosão selvática das cores que consomem hipotéticas respirações Até dos objectos de uso diário cerâmicas vestuário em arranjos formais de padrão característico Ornamentações em elipse curva círculo e zi-

guezague sobrecarregando a nostalgia do clã Envolto nos estigmas do medo e da esperança Que espreitam sobre o ombro de Malangatana e o visitam quando baixo a guarda Entra em transe e pinta os visitantes De dois mundos distintos que se socorrem mutuamente O vivenciado que o seu coração alberga e aquele a que ele próprio e o seu povo aspiram Um breve grito de liberdade encima a composição rasgando uma abertura ao sonho e uma multivivência caótica a enovelar-se sobre si "Falta o ar" mas tudo é vivo e dialoga e canta Se comprime e jamais liberta Movendo-se Nos mundos a enlaçarem sedimentos de crenças seculares Representados por realidades míticas e fetichistas Registam uma multidão anónima de rostos abismados na tortura da existência em condições precárias Que se anulam face à condução mágica dos destinos Actores e assistentes de acontecimentos terríveis Veneram o culto dos poderes sobrenaturais Evocam antepassados Predizem tragédias Mitificam o amor Velam os ódios Cegam na eficácia dos exorcismos Param à espera do tempo Caldeiam os actos triviais com preocupações do além Um estranho erotismo emana dessa sufocação Uma rede apertada tece a angústia A alegria de existir e a amargura de viver cerram-se em comunhão Como é rico e imaginativo o tecido que forra o espírito de Malangatana O seu discurso narrativo privilegia as mulheres as crianças o bicho-homem e o bicho-bicho Ele simboliza o espírito da agressão com unhas e dentes Apela ao naufrágio no oceano leitoso dos olhares Faz da pintura uma bandeira de denúncia das condições de vida de um povo sofredor Com um expressionismo dramático e lírico como se a sua voz mais inexplorada se destinasse à pira da loucura Representa o amor o ódio a vida e a morte com a sabedoria emblemática do mestre Transforma os humanos em seres híbridos que constrói como símbolos duma África reprimida que a sua paleta universaliza Na dilatação das pupilas No agigantamento das mãos Na sacralização das máscaras Na vigilância dos mochos Nas imponentes garras e bicos das águias Nos dentes finos dos peixes No caos e no labirinto Donde renasce a estridência crepitante das fogueiras primitivas Para que ele hoje tal como algures no passado dance excessivamente à roda do fogo Puxando os espíritos do Bem e do Saber para que se não volte a afivelar o sacrifício dos inocentes E a todo o instante em cada nova tela renasça o espírito universal do homem Cante o seu povo e o liberte Certeira e lentamente Como convém ao Eterno

Margarida Santos
Canelas, December, 1993

O que mais me surpreende e fascina nas poderosas pinturas de Malangatana é a sua força interpelativa. São francas: carecem de toda a duplicidade da ironia e de todo o esfumado do sonhado. São directas, mas não à maneira da efusão intempestiva, e sim do assalto largamente premeditado. São também abertamente eloquentes: as cores e as formas, os traços e pinceladas e os ritmos desprendem, no seu conflito veemente, o corpo palpável de um cântico agressivo ou de uma fala encantatória a que nos podemos subtrair. [...]

Pablo Oyarzún Robles

In the exhibition catalogue, Santiago, Chile, 1994

gatana continuará com todas as suas cargas emocionais, com toda a sua carga de paixão, só que agora não provocadas pela morte, a destruição e o ódio. As tensões provocadoras poderão ser essencialmente de Amor.

Júlio Navarro

In the exhibition catalogue, Macau, 1996

Ambas fascinantes. Ambas carregadas de paixão — sim, porque a pessoa, embora sobre um exterior calmo, é um fervilhar de emoções. Aliás se não o fosse como surgiriam as suas apaixonadas obras, espelhando sempre a situação que ele e o seu povo vivem? E, conscientemente ou não — e quer-me parecer que só raras vezes a sua obra é totalmente dirigida —, surgem o adensar das cores, a intensidade da composição, ou o aclarar de algumas zonas e a abertura de um espaço — a esperança que nele reside.— Ao vermos os seus trabalhos expostos nesta sua 1.ª individual de Pintura em Moçambique pós-Independência, que nos traz obras desde 1992 até às de hoje, podemos notar bem o facto. Malangatana nas obras recentes avança numa paleta de cores muito mais aberta. A tensão das suas telas deixa de ser dramática. Propositadamente ou não isto não corresponderá ao facto de o Autor já se encontrar num País em Paz? Não se deverá, a já ser possível, ir à mítica Matalana e até pensar para ela projectos futuros? Não se deverá poder sonhar outra vez um Moçambique a desenvolver-se como o estava antes da guerra?

É esta capacidade de usar artisticamente as suas cargas emocionais que sempre tem dado força especial à sua obra. Desde os primeiros trabalhos de aparência naiv até aos elaboradíssimos de hoje, a mesma força sempre neles tem latejado — talvez também resida aí o facto de ser o único artista naiv — de que eu tenha conhecimento — que passou de naiv a artista dito erudito — passe a etiqueta —, mantendo uma mesma qualidade. A esta força e também talvez porque — e devido a ela — de naiv só tinha a aparência superficial.

Poderíamos sentir que, desaparecendo as grandes tensões anteriores que foram as pulsões fundamentais da sua obra, esta passaria a correr perigo numa situação de acalmia. Já podemos ver que não, e, embora talvez sem o dramatismo, o Homem Malan-

As tensões que sempre fizeram e viveram nas obras de Malangatana não têm de ser as causadas pela opressão colonial e o tratamento dado ao seu povo no antigamente e pela guerra devastadora que foi movida ao seu povo, destruindo as famílias, matando milhares de crianças.

Elas podem ser pela pulsão do amor, pelo desencadear de Eros, por toda a força despoletada por estas intensas pulsões que fazem ressaltar as mesmas violências, apaixonadas mas não necessariamente anuladoras do ser humano. Se tivéssemos dúvidas aí está "Canto a Eros" a demonstrá-lo.

Aliás, se virmos a obra de Malangatana, desde sempre estas outras pulsões a atravessaram, desde sempre estas tensões que a atravessam se confundiram com as de violência destruidora, misturando-se às vezes de tal forma, que difícil seria dizer se os *monstros* que o povoavam provinham da violência da morte.

Este conjunto de 30 desenhos e aguarelas ainda não mostrados em público que hoje aqui se nos apresentam constituem um poderoso confirmar de que Malangatana quando canta Eros nada perde da sua intensidade, da sua força e da sua beleza, do seu trabalho por vezes de um delirante barroquismo ou mantendo um despojar de formas em que até o aparente inacabar de um desenho é a necessidade de reforçar esta intensidade, o fazer este pulsar erótico tornar-se mais forte. Ou ainda, como naquele pequeno *monstrozinho*, esta tensão exprime-se apenas por um *sentir* de que a sua forma, o seu ordenamento de traços, a subtileza de alguns detalhes, nos deixam aperceber o latejar de Eros. [...]

The Friends of the National Museum of Art, in the "Song to Eros" catalogue, 1996

Malangatana: A Biography

Malangatana (Valente Ngwenya) was born on June 6, 1936, in Matalana, Maputo Province, Mozambique.

He attended primary school in Matalana, and, later, the first years of the trade school in Maputo.

He was a herder of cattle, an apprentice to a nyamussoro (traditional healer), a nanny, a ball boy and servant at an elite club in colonial Lourenço Marques.

He became a professional artist in 1960, thanks to the support of the Portuguese architect Miranda (Pancho) Guedes, who gave him a garage for a studio and bought two paintings per month at a price higher than what a black servant such as he could earn.

Accused of ties to FRELIMO, he was imprisoned by the colonial police in a roundup which also put the poets José Craveirinha (winner of the Camões Prize) and Rui Nogar, now deceased, in jail.

In contrast to his companions, he ended up being acquitted for lack of proof of the alleged involvement after almost 2 years in prison.

Nevertheless, the pressure he felt was always expressed in his paintings, which conveyed their meanings very clearly in spite of not using realistic portraiture. His works of that time all show symbolic denunciation of the oppression of the blacks. After Independence he acted in various political roles, he was a FRELIMO deputy from 1990 until he stepped down in 1994 at the time of the first multiparty elections.

Today he is one of FRELIMO's members in the Maputo Municipal Assembly, elected on June 30, 1998.

He was one of the founders of the Peace Movement, and on the Board of Directors for the Boy Scouts of Mozambique.

He was one of the creators of the National Museum of Art of Mozambique and has been a supporter, and guiding light, for the Núcleo de Arte (a cooperative for painters and sculptors).

Very supportive of children, he has collaborated intensely with UNICEF, and for several years ran a Sunday playschool for children in his neighbourhood called "Vamos Brincar" (Let's Play).

Many years ago he spearheaded the founding of a cultural project for his native village — Matalana, Marracuene — and, as soon as the war ended, formed the Association for Matalana's Cultural Centre, of which he is currently serving as president. The association plans to create an integrated development programme for the villagers, with professional development and self-employment projects, together with artistic work and ethnographic, anthropological and ecologic collections.

Since 1959 he has participated in group exhibits all over the world, in addition to Mozambique, including South Africa, Angola, Brazil, Bulgaria, Czechoslovakia, Cuba, Denmark, Spain, the United States, Finland, France, Great Britain, Holland, India, Iceland, Italy, Nigeria, Norway, Pakistan, Portugal, the German Democratic Republic, Rhodesia, Sweden, the Soviet Union and Zimbabwe.

Since 1961 he had had innumerable solo exhibits internationally, in Germany, Austria, Bulgaria, Chile, Cuba, the United States, Spain, India, Macau, Portugal and Turkey, in addition to within Mozambique.

He has painted murals and incised cement walls in various areas of Maputo and the city of Beira, in Mozambique, and in South Africa, Chile, Colombia, the United States, Great Britain, Swaziland and Sweden. In addition to the murals and two open-air iron sculptures, the collection of his artistic work (paintings, drawings, watercolours, prints, ceramics, tapestry, sculpture) is found — in addition to the artist's vast personal collection — in museums and public galleries, as well as private collections, in many parts of the world.

A member of the first jury for the UNESCO Prize to promote the arts; a permanent member of the "Heritage" jury in Zimbabwe; a member of the jury for the second Biennale of Havana; member of the jury for the International Children's Art Exposition of Moscow; member of the jury for various artistic events in Mozambique; National Vice-Chairman for Culture for Mozambique's participation in Expo '98.

Malangatana beside President Samora Machel at the inauguration of his retrospective exhibit in Maputo, 1986

Chronology of Artistic Activity

1959
Participates in 3 group exhibitions in Lourenço Marques

1961
Solo exhibition in Lourenço Marques
Participates in a group exhibition in Cape Town

1962-1964
Participates in group exhibitions in Mozambique,
        South Africa, Angola, France, India,
        Nigeria, Pakistan and Rhodesia
Solo exhibition of drawings at the UN in New York

1966-1970
Gulbenkian Foundation scholarship to study ceramics
        and printmaking in Portugal
Participates in group exhibitions in Paris

1972
Two exhibits simultaneously in Lisbon
Solo exhibit of drawings, ceramics and prints in
        Lourenço Marques
Participates in group exhibitions in Mozambique
        and Czechoslovakia

1973-1974
Participates in group exhibitions in Mozambique,
        Soweto and Washington
Solo exhibition of drawings in Portugal

1975-1984
Participates in group exhibitions in Mozambique,
        Angola, Brazil (tapestries), Bulgaria, Cuba,
        France, Great Britain, Holland, Italy, Nigeria,
        Portugal, German Democratic Republic,
        Sweden, USSR and Zimbabwe

1984
Exhibition with the sculptor Chissano in New Delhi
Takes part in "International Artists Against
        Apartheid," exhibiting in various cities
        of Sweden, Finland and Denmark

1985
Solo exhibit of painting and solo exhibit of drawings
        in Portugal
Participates in group exhibits in Mozambique
"International Artists Against Apartheid,"
        tours various European cities

1986
Retrospective in Maputo
A much smaller retrospective is exhibited in several
        German cities and at the II Biennale
        of Havana
Participates in group exhibits in Mozambique

1987-1989
The small version of the retrospective is exhibited
        in Bulgaria and Austria
Participates in group exhibits in Mozambique,
        Great Britain, Norway and Sweden
Exhibition with the sculptor Chissano in Ankara

1989
Retrospective in Lisbon
Construction of large iron and cement sculpture
        (15 metres) in Infulene, Mozambique

1990
Solo exhibit of drawings in Lisbon
Participates in group exhibits in Mozambique

1991
Participates in "Africa Explores" which tours
        various cities in the US
Exhibition with Idasse in several cities of Portugal

1992
"Africa Explores" continues to tour several US cities
Participates in group exhibits in Mozambique
        and at Expo '92 in Seville where he paints
        the façade of the African pavilion

1993
"Africa Explores" continues to tour several US
        cities and goes to France
Participates in group exhibits in Mozambique
Solo exhibition of drawings in Maputo

1994
"Africa Explores" continues to tour several
        European cities
Participates in group exhibits in Maputo
        and Cape Town
Solo exhibition of paintings in Santiago, Chile,
        and in Maputo
Resumed work on iron and cement sculpture
        in Infulene

Malangatana prepares to attack a good-sized canvas

The exterior of Malangatana's house — designed by "Pancho" Miranda Guedes, with works in iron, tiles and bas-reliefs by the artist

1995
"Africa Explores" continues to tour several
       European cities
Participates in group exhibits in Maputo
Finishes (?) the iron and cement sculpture in Infulene,
       which has grown to 20 metres in height

1996
"Africa Explores" continues to tour several European
       cities
Participates in group exhibits in Maputo, Lisbon,
       Termoli, Finland and Copenhagen
       ("Container '96")
Solo exhibition of drawings and watercolours,
       "Canto a Eros" ("Song to Eros") in Maputo
Solo exhibit of war drawings in Lisbon
Solo exhibit of paintings in Macau
Participation in a workshop in Termoli

1997
Participates in group exhibits in Maputo, Finland,
       Lisbon and Moscow
Solo exhibit in Sintra, Portugal
Painted mural for UNESCO

1998
Participates in group exhibits in Maputo,
       Brazil and Lisbon (one was at Expo '98)
Exhibition with Estevao Mucavel in Reykjavik
Invited to the World Festival of Poetry
       in Medellin and solo exhibit in that city
Creates a mobile sculpture and a mural panel
       in the Mozambican pavilion for Expo '98

Two views of Malangatana's studio. The *Black Christ*, painted during Nelson Mandela's imprisonment, is seen in the photograph on the right

Prizes and Honours

1959
Honourable Mention in the 1st Fine Arts Competition, Lourenço Marques

1962
1st prize for Painting, "Festival of Lourenço Marques"

1968
2nd prize for Painting (*ex-aequo*), "Festival of July 24th", Lourenço Marques

1970
Diploma and Medal of Merit, Romase Campanella Academy of Arts and Sciences, Italy

1984
Nachingwea Medal for contributions to Mozambican culture

1990
Prize from the International Association of Art Critics, Lisbon

1995
Grand Official of the Order of the Infante D. Henrique, Portugal

1997
Prince Claus Prize, the Netherlands

Index of Titles

Contents